Charles L Holland

DEVOTIONAL REFLECTIONS
on the
Teachings of Jesus
from the Four Gospels

Charles Lee Holland, Jr.

Copyright © 2021 Charles Lee Holland, Jr.

All rights reserved. No part of this book may be used or reproduced by any means, graphic, electronic, or mechanical, including photocopying, recording, taping or by any information storage retrieval system without the written permission of the author except in the case of brief quotations embodied in critical articles and reviews.

WestBow Press books may be ordered through booksellers or by contacting:

WestBow Press
A Division of Thomas Nelson & Zondervan
1663 Liberty Drive
Bloomington, IN 47403
www.westbowpress.com
844-714-3454

Because of the dynamic nature of the Internet, any web addresses or links contained in this book may have changed since publication and may no longer be valid. The views expressed in this work are solely those of the author and do not necessarily reflect the views of the publisher, and the publisher hereby disclaims any responsibility for them.

Any people depicted in stock imagery provided by Getty Images are models, and such images are being used for illustrative purposes only. Certain stock imagery © Getty Images.

[Scripture quotations are] from the New Revised Standard Version Bible, copyright © 1989 the Division of Christian Education of the National Council of the Churches of Christ in the United States of America. Used by permission. All rights reserved.

ISBN: 978-1-6642-2157-4 (sc)
ISBN: 978-1-6642-2159-8 (hc)
ISBN: 978-1-6642-2158-1 (e)

Library of Congress Control Number: 2021901921

Print information available on the last page.

WestBow Press rev. date: 02/19/2021

REMEMBERING

Furman Judson Nolen
Aug. 29, 1885–May 5, 1956
Grandfather – Mentor – Friend

CONTENTS

Preface xi

PART ONE
The Gospel of Matthew

4:10	Christian Worship	1
4:18–22	Christian Discipleship	3
5:13–16	Christian Responsibility	5
5:39–44	The Law of Love	7
6:14–15	Forgiveness	9
6:25–26	Why Worry?	11
7:12	The Ethics of Jesus	13
16:15–18	Christ's Church	15
24:35–37, 44	Jesus Is Coming Again	17
6:7–10	Our Father in Heaven	19
27:45–46	Why?	21
28:18–20	Christianity in the Active Tense	23

PART TWO
The Gospel of Mark

1:14–15	The Gospel	27
1:16–20	Who ... Me?	29
2:1–12	Forgiveness	31
4:21–25	To Those Who Have, More Will Be Given .	33
4:35–41	Signs and Wonders	35
7:14–23	Positive Desires	37

7:38–44	A Lesson in Tolerance	39
9:42–48	Self-Control	41
10:17–22	Redemptive Curiosity	43
11:20–24	Faith in God	45
12:28–31	Love – The Great Commandment	47

PART THREE

The Gospel of Luke

1:30–25	Jesus: God and Man?	51
2:8–11	Good News for You	53
4:16–19	To Make Christ Known	55
5:27–32	A Strange Paradox	57
7:36–50	To Whom Little Is Forgiven	59
9:57–62	Radical Discipleship	61
10:25–28	The Imperative of Love	63
12:16–21	Understanding Life	65
13:18–19	Little Is Big When God Is in It	67
14:15–24	Invitation to Life	69
15:11–24	On Being Yourself	71
17:7–10	Authentic Humility	73
23:32–38	The Way to Perfect Health	75
23:39–43	The Great Promise	77
24:46–48	The Gauntlet of the Galilean	79

PART FOUR

The Gospel of John

1:9–13	Tomorrow's Christian	83
1:14–18	How to See God	85

1:35–42	Discipleship: Mystery and Goal	87
3:16–17	God's Grace in Action	89
3:25–36	The Life of Jesus in the Life of the Believer	91
4:1–26	All Is Not Lost	93
4:7–38	True Worship	95
5:1–8	On the Desire of the Heart	97
6:35–40	Jesus: The Bread of Life	99
7:37–39	Cordial Invitation	101
8:1–11	The Loving God	103
8:34–59	The Quest for Truth	105
10:11–18	Community	107
10:7–10	The Rediscovery of Christian Vitality	109
11:17–44	I Can Face Tomorrow	111
12:1–8	The Absence of Jesus	113
13:1–20	The Cross and the Towel	115
14:1–14	Immortal Longings	117
14:25–27	Christ's Peace	119
15:1–17	How to Choose a Friend	121
16:12–15	The Spirit of Truth	123
16:29–33	Victory in Jesus	125
17:1–5	Eternal Life	127
17:1–5	Eternal Life II	129
18:33–38	Truth	131
19:12–16	King of Kings	133
19:16–25	The Cross of Christ	135
19:28–30	Human Needs	137
20:19–23	The Christian and Missions	139
20:19–29	Honest Skepticism	141

Preface

The purpose of this book of devotional reflections is to enable the reader to appropriate, assimilate, and apply the words of Christ to the challenges of daily living. Further, it is the author's desire that a clearer understanding may be achieved of how the words of this ancient book are pertinent to the rapidly evolving issues emerging in the twenty-first century. In the process of reading the commentaries presented, many answers to current questions will be evident to those who are eager to hear a fresh word from the Lord. Indeed, the teachings of Jesus remain God's word to all people. In addition, one may note that the questions raised in the book are equally provocative as the answers given.

In the present endeavor, consideration is limited to some of the teachings of Jesus as found in the four gospels of Matthew, Mark, Luke, and John. Accordingly, one may realize that the material as presented will enhance personal devotion time as well as make possible informative and inspiring group or class study.

The book, *Devotional Reflections*, is based on the singular conviction of the divine inspiration of the scriptures. This conviction derives directly from 2 Timothy 3:16–17: "All scripture is inspired by God and is useful for teaching, for reproof, for correction, and for training in righteousness, so that everyone who belongs to God may be proficient, equipped for every good work." Consequently, this book is an invitation for us to hear once again the winsome words of Jesus of Nazareth, knowing that we are listening to the Word of God for us.

CLH
Fort Worth, Texas
Summer 2020

PART ONE

THE GOSPEL OF
MATTHEW

Christian Worship

Jesus said: "It is written, 'Worship the Lord your God.'" (Matthew 4:10)

Abraham Heschel, the great Jewish religious leader, made an observation beneficial to Jews and Christians alike: "God may be of no concern to man, but man is of much concern to God. The only way to discover this is the ultimate way, the way of worship. For worship is a way of living, a way of seeing the world in the light of God."

In what form does Christian worship manifest those distinctive qualities that make it truly Christian in nature? Through the centuries, two elements have continued together. They are the preaching and hearing of the Word, and the celebration of the Eucharist (the Lord's supper). Although they differ in actual presentation, one being spoken and the other being acted, they are identical in their essential function. They both exist to proclaim the gospel of Christ's redeeming grace in all its power and glory.

So the command remains: "You shall worship the Lord your God." Why? Worship is the dynamic, personal involvement of the Christian in the kingdom of God. In other words, our worship here is a faint echo of the celebration in heaven.

Questions for Reflection

- At times, do you feel that you are of no concern to God or anyone else?
- What effort have you made to remedy the problem?
- Have you considered talking it over with a friend?
- Have you sought the help of a professional counselor?
- Most important, have you discussed the matter with God?
- Have you given worship a chance in your life? When and with what frequency?

Christian Discipleship

As he walked by the Sea of Galilee, he saw two brothers, Simon, who is called Peter, and Andrew his brother, casting nets into the sea—for they were fishermen. And he said to them, "Follow me, and I will make you fish for people." Immediately they left their nets and followed him. As he went from there, he saw two other brothers, James son of Zebedee and his brother John, in the boat with their father Zebedee, mending their nets, and he called them. Immediately they left their boat and their father, and followed him. (Matthew 4:18–22)

Surely it is true that Christian discipleship is a new way of acting and thinking. Such discipleship is quite radical, for it allows only for a solitary affection, and that affection is for Christ. We must never allow anything to come between Christ and ourselves. The true disciple looks first and primarily to God. Other entities retain interest and concern, but it is Christ who remains primary in the life of the true disciple.

Such radical discipleship is experienced only by those who possess a radical love for Jesus. The "follow me" that Jesus asked of his disciples was never supported by any rationalization. Thus, the response of the disciples was not that of admiration based on logical reasons but rather complete devotion based on love. They did not follow him because of what he said, but they followed him because of who he was. That principle remains valid for us today. We can follow his teachings only after we follow him. We can never fully believe in the truth as presented in the Sermon on the Mount unless we first believe in the preacher on the mount.

Questions for Reflection

- To get right to the point, Lord, are you calling me to follow you?
- If so, I am confronted with a problem! The world is in a mess because I have made a mess in the world. Do you still want me to help you in the world?
- Is my commitment to Christ real? Am I able to give him my love, my heart, my mind, and my life?
- Am I truly willing? God, help me to become a true disciple.

Christian Responsibility

> You are the salt of the earth; but if salt has lost its taste, how can its saltiness be restored? It is no longer good for anything, but is thrown out and trampled under foot.
>
> You are the light of the world. A city built on a hill cannot be hid. No one after lighting a lamp puts it under the bushel basket, but on the lampstand and it gives light to all in the house. In the same way, let your light shine before others, so that they may see your good works and give glory to your Father in heaven. (Matthew 5:13–16)

In a famous speech delivered to the Central Committee of the Communist Party on February 14, 1956, Nikita Khrushchev observed, "A Communist has no right to be a mere onlooker." If that is true of a Communist, it is infinitely more true of a Christian.

A basic tenet of the Bible is personal responsibility. The Christian is responsible to do something positive in a world that is subjected to the influence of negative forces. A dynamic Christian life is far more socially redemptive than formal governmental legislation. The Christian has an opportunity to apply in a practical way the principles of the gospel to the problems of today. Further, the Christian is responsible to do so.

At the dawn of the Christian era, Jesus delivered a sermon in which he declared, "You are the light of the world!" Since then we have known that a Christian has no right to be a mere onlooker.

Questions for Reflection

- Is my relationship with Christ really a priority in my life?
- Or, like my club or lodge membership, is it just one more social function with a measure of busy work to check off each Sunday?
- Should there be in my life a strong element of urgency?
- Meditate on Hebrews 6:10, which says, "God is not unjust; he will not overlook your work and the love you showed for his sake in serving the saints, as you still do."

The Law of Love

But if anyone strikes you on the right cheek, turn the other also. ... Love your enemies ....
(Matthew 5:39, 44)

Are we to interpret this passage literally, or shall we seek some redemptive principle that will have practical value in daily life? If we take it literally, those who perpetuate violence in our land may expect an unchallenged field day as they proceed to work their mischief. We must not misunderstand the intent of the biblical revelation.

First, let us clear the air of misunderstanding. The Christian faith does not advocate nonresistance in the instance of unprovoked violence. Rather, Jesus is introducing a new principle into the rigid legal system of the Old Testament. He addresses the law of retaliation—"An eye for an eye, and a tooth for a tooth" (Exodus 21:23–25)—with his new way of reconciliation, the law of love.

While we should protect our loved ones and ourselves, we are to rise above the level of like retaliation. How is such an approach actualized? Usually it is achieved with considerable effort. However, we may try such simple measures as ignoring verbal insults, honestly striving to forgive the presumed wrongs done to us, and practicing a gracious and generous spirit to everyone.

Questions for Reflection

- Have you been hurt by someone recently?
- Was it physical or emotional in nature?
- How did you respond? How are you responding now?
- Did you get mad? Or get even? Or both?
- After reflection, how would you change your response, if it were possible to do so?

Forgiveness

> If you forgive their trespasses, your heavenly Father will also forgive you; but if you do not forgive others, neither will your Father forgive your trespasses. (Matthew 6:14–15)

Forgiveness is such a grand theme that it is almost beyond our ability to contemplate it. The difficulty is made greater by the fact that so many of us retain a harsh and unforgiving spirit toward others. That, indeed, is sad, for as George Herbert puts it, "He who cannot forgive breaks the bridge over which he himself must pass."

It is a central truth of the Bible that the singular way to the new life in Christ is forgiveness. In God's forgiveness, we are invited out of the arena of divine judgment and into the arms of divine love. This new life within God's love opens to us a release from fear and failure. Thus, we are welcomed into the new life of faith, hope, and love.

Forgiveness is the gentle breeze of God. It is breathed in and breathed out. The person who has truly inhaled the forgiveness of God is enabled to exhale forgiveness to others. Surely that was the idea of Jesus when he taught his disciples to pray accordingly: "And forgive us our debts as we forgive our debtors."

Questions for Reflection

- Consider your relationship with other persons, especially certain persons who have hurt you in some manner.
- Have you settled the matter in your heart?
- Perhaps their hurting you was a reaction on their part to some action from you toward them?
- Have you dealt with your own motives, attitudes, and actions?
- Have you asked for and received God's forgiveness?
- If so, you may now consider inviting the other person back into your life, assuring him or her of your forgiveness from God and toward him or her.

Why Worry?

> Therefore I tell you, do not worry about your life, what you will eat or what you will drink, or about your body, what you will wear. Is not life more than food, and the body more than clothing? Look at the birds of the air; they neither sow nor reap nor gather into barns, and yet your heavenly Father feeds them. Are you not of more value than they? (Matthew 6:25–26)

We often hear people say "public enemy number one." This term is usually associated with some infamous criminal who is being sought by law enforcement agents across the nation. However, it may be that the public enemy number one is not personalized to that degree. It may be that you are having to cope with this enemy yourself. Worry is likely the greatest enemy that we confront in our everyday living.

We all worry. Some of us worry more than others. Essentially, worry is inherent in the human nature. Anxiety, frustration, and a sense of insecurity are all motivators for the human personality to react by worrying. Then along comes this strange directive from our Lord, "Do not worry!" St. Paul provides the identical counsel: "Do not worry about anything" (Philippians 4:6).

That is easy to say, but it is difficult to achieve. As a matter of fact, we cannot achieve this objective within ourselves. Again, Paul provides the answer for which we are seeking: "but in everything by prayer and supplication with thanksgiving make your request known to God. And the peace of God which passes all understanding shall keep your hearts and minds through Christ" (Philippians 4:6–7).

Questions for Reflection

- Are you given to worrying? A great deal?
- Review five things that frequently cause you to worry.
- Now read once more the last quotation from Philippians. Did you carefully read it? Do you believe it works?
- A very important question for you: *Have you tried it?*
- In contemporary plain talk, the prescription for your malady is quite clear and accessible: Submit your worries to the therapy of prayer. Follow this prescription daily, and you are a recovering and even a healed worrier.

The Ethics of Jesus

> In everything do to others as you would have them do to you; for this is the law and the prophets. (Matthew 7:12)

What relationship has the teachings of a first-century carpenter with our modern times? It sems incredible that such ancient concepts should have any contemporary relevance! The thinking person may wish to question whether the idioms, maxims, and principles laid down by Jesus will work in today's world.

The essential stuff of humankind is forever the same. Obviously, the external trappings of life vary from age to age and generation to generation. Still, the primary features of human existence remain consistent. In a way, it may be stated that man is timeless. Since it is to mankind that the teachings are addressed, it is certain that those teachings are timeless.

Every person of every era is faced with the task of establishing meaningful and pertinent priorities. Likewise, each person is tempted to glide, drift, and embrace the easy, convenient, profitable, and pleasurable course of action. Just as Jesus knew of our natural tendency, he also knew of our spiritual potential. Therefore, he bequeathed to us The Golden Rule, the basis of true ethical living.

Questions for Reflection

- To what extent are the ethical teachings of Jesus guiding my daily thoughts and actions?
- Is my lifestyle reflective of the concepts and directives of Jesus?
- In my interpersonal relationships, as I deal with daily issues, do I ever pause to pose the question, "What would Jesus do or say in this situation?"
- To be specific, how may the Christian of today apply the ethics of Jesus to such social issues as race relations, equal justice for all persons, and the existence of prejudice, intolerance and religious and ethnic diversity?

Christ's Church

He said to them, "But who do you say that I am?" Simon Peter answered, "You are the Messiah, the Son of the Living God." And Jesus answered him, "Blessed are you Simon son of Jonah! For flesh and blood has not revealed this to you, but my Father in heaven. And I tell you, you are Peter, and on this rock I will build my church, and the gates of Hades will not prevail against it." (Matthew 16:15–18)

Jesus observed, "I will build my church." Those are revealing words. For one thing, the existence of the church is dependent upon Christ. Try as we may, our best efforts are futile when it comes to establishing the church of Jesus Christ. Thus, the origin of the church is Jesus.

Next, there is the certainty of the project. Jesus proclaimed, "I will …." These are days of uncertainty and confusion in many areas of life. However, in the area of Christ's intention there is positive certainty. The reality of Christ's church as a redemptive factor in human society is a foregone conclusion because of the promise of Jesus.

Finally, it is essential for us to mark with care the ownership of the church. Jesus referred to it as "my church." The leader of the church is Christ. The authority of the church is Christ. The judge of the church is Christ. The Savior of the church is Christ. The Lord of the church is Christ. In a word, if the church is Christ's church, it is somewhat inaccurate to refer to it as "our church."

Questions for Reflection

- Do you find yourself bewildered by the frequent confusion and disputation that occurs in local congregations and in denominations as well?
- Do you often find yourself crying out, "Does it have to be this way?"
- Perhaps the correct question for you to ask is "Who is in charge of this church anyway?"
- As a Christian and a member of a church myself, it may be appropriate for me to ask whether I am willing in actual practice to surrender to Christ the spiritual and practical direction of this church.
- Christ is Lord of his church. Therefore, let us listen to the leading of his ever-present Spirit.

Jesus Is Coming Again

> But about that day and hour no one knows, neither the angels of heaven, nor the Son, but only the Father. For as the days of Noah were, so will be the coming of the Son of Man.
>
> Therefore, you also must be ready, for the Son of Man is coming at an unexpected hour. (Matthew 24:35–37, 44)

Christians live in the tension between waiting and coming—our waiting and Christ's coming. What about this waiting? Actually, waiting is a very intriguing word within itself. It involves the process of having and not having at the same time. When used in the context of the Christian hope of ultimate redemption, it involves the experience of not having, not seeing, and not actually realizing.

Nevertheless, waiting is also having. We know as a result of our own experience that in great measure realization is part anticipation. Who among us would surrender the month before Christmas with its carols, lights, and frantic parties, and have only the day itself? We have learned that those who wait in patience (sometimes in impatience) are already in the grip of that for which they wait.

Where does this leave us as we struggle along in the tension between waiting and coming? Well, it leaves us expecting our Lord to come for each of us at one time or another, or all of us together at one time or another. Until then, we shall continue waiting and watching, working and praying. Even if we do not have our Lord in all his glory today, we do have him, for we are grasped by the certainty that he is coming. So we wait, for it is our destiny to wait. But we wait in the full knowledge that our waiting moves inevitably nearer the event when time becomes eternity, and our coming Lord shall have fully and finally come.

Questions for Reflection

- ➤ Perhaps this is a moment for being honest with ourselves. Therefore, do you often think seriously regarding the ultimate matters of your life and its culmination?
- ➤ What about the end of the world as we know it today?
- ➤ What do you think about the "blessed hope" of the Christian that Jesus will return to receive his own and establish the kingdom of God upon this earth?
- ➤ If you really believe in heaven and eternal life, do the material and secular matters of life concern you all that much?
- ➤ About this "waiting and watching" for the Second Coming, consider where you give the majority of your time, effort, interest and financial resources.

Our Father in Heaven

When you are praying, do not heap up empty phrases as the Gentiles do; for they think they will be heard because of their many words. Do not be like them, for your Father knows what you need before you ask him.

Pray then this way:

> Our Father in heaven,
> hallowed be your name.
> Your kingdom come,
> Your will be done,
> on earth as it is in heaven." (Matthew 6:7–10)

The word *Father* was a favorite term of Jesus and others in the New Testament. It continues to be one of the most frequently employed symbols until this very day. There are several reasons for this.

First, the word *Father* expresses a human relationship that immediately communicates clearly understood concepts. Familiar affections, obligations, hopes and fears are readily applicable to the divine-human relationship when God is referred to as *Father*.

Second, the term *Father* allows the retention of the basic sense of awe and reverence for God, which is an inherent quality in all people. The overarching sovereignty of God is kept intact, thus allowing each of us to respond in humility, obedience and worship.

Third, the dignity of humanity is an essential component in the Father-child image. If God is indeed the Father, then we, as his children, are supplied the ground for adequate self-respect, dignity, and individual fulfillment.

And finally, the resulting relationship of communion and fellowship is assured. The Father loves the child and acts in grace, mercy, and love. He also chastens and corrects, but this is always in the context of love. And this is the heart of the Judeo-Christian faith: He is our Father, and we are his children, and we know we have access to Him, security with him, and salvation in him.

Questions for Reflection

- Do you feel that you know God, really know him?
- Do you feel close to God?
- Do you often share in a conversation with him? That is, pray intimately with your Father?
- To what extent are you and the Father good friends?
- In what ways do you think that your relationship with the Father might be improved? How can you make a difference? Think about it.

Why?

> From noon on, darkness came over the whole land until three in the afternoon. And about three o'clock Jesus cried with a loud voice, ... "My God, my God, why have you forsaken me?" (Matthew 27:45–46)

Jesus died without understanding why. If he had understood, he would not have asked the question, or it would have been a foolish prayer. He died without understanding why. The interpretation for that suffering came later as the apostle Paul, writing to the church in Corinth, said, "For our sake he made him to be sin who knew no sin, so that in him we might become the righteousness of God" (2 Corinthians 5:21). That was why. And God gave the answer *through* Jesus, and not to Jesus.

The power of faith is related to the story of a God who loves us so much that he took us into his feeling, into his concern, into his suffering. Indeed, God took us into the depth of his feeling and into the depth of his concern to the point that we desire to stop asking the question "Why?" and become partners with him in his suffering.

Questions for Reflection

- Why do we struggle with so many unresolved questions?
- Have you ever heard someone say, "You must never question God"? Remember, Jesus did!
- If Jesus is our example, why should we not have the same freedom?
- Do you have some questions pertaining to your own situation in life that you would like to ask God?
- If so, then ask him. Jesus did.

Christianity in the Active Tense

And Jesus came and said to them, "All authority in heaven and on earth has been given to me. Go therefore, and make disciples of all nations, baptizing them in the name of the Father and of the Son and of the Holy Spirit, and teaching them to obey everything that I have commanded you. And remember, I am with you always, to the end of the age." (Matthew 28:18–20)

We hear a great deal these days about active and inactive Christians. At times, it seems that there are more of the inactive kind than one might expect. We have large membership rolls and relatively few members who truly are involved in any meaningful way in the redemptive ministries of the church. As we all know, we are given to counting numbers rather than making numbers count. What is our problem?

For one thing, most of us prefer to serve the Lord on our own terms rather than his. It is impossible to do the work of God on the basis of human reason and strength. Therefore, we must realize the importance of serving the Lord on his terms. It is not as if his terms were vague and obscure. Indeed, they are clear and particular. Essentially, Christ's terms are simply stated in these familiar lines:

> Go therefore and make disciples of all nations, baptizing them in the name of the Father and of the Son and of the Holy Spirit, teaching them to obey all that I have commanded you. (Matthew 28:19– 20)

One matter is very evident. The Christianity of the New Testament is best translated in the active tense.

Questions for Reflection

- Why do you suppose that many of us Christians are intimidated by the secular world in which we live?
- Why are we reluctant to bear an aggressive witness for Christ?
- On the occasion when we find ourselves speaking of our relationship with Christ, do we proclaim it, or do we merely admit it with measured timidity?
- In our prayers, how do we explain or confess to God our failure to be an active witness for him in word and way of life?
- Does the issue of the active versus the passive witness rest on the matter of love? In other words, if I loved others, the world, as God loves, would I not gladly share that love with whomever from wherever?

PART TWO

THE GOSPEL OF
MARK

The Gospel

> Now after John was arrested, Jesus came to Galilee, proclaiming the gospel of God, and saying, "The time is fulfilled, and the kingdom of God has come near; repent and believe in the gospel." (Mark 1:14–15)

The gospel is the essence of reality and must be understood as such. It is an unblinking reflection of everyday life. Accordingly, therefore, the gospel avoids any sort of saccharine approach to life, death, and eternity that may result in a bland, soft-boiled hope of little substance and no validity. Indeed, the gospel confronts the tragedy of human failure with the amazing and provocative prescription of divine love mixed with sensorial sacrifice; and taken reverently by faith. The results are inevitable: salvation now and forever.

Because of inherent human pride, the gospel frequently is a difficult pill to swallow. This is true because the gospel, usually referred to as the Good News, is always bad news before it is good news. Before it tells us of the great salvation available for us, it informs us that we are lost sinners. Such incriminating information is difficult to accept.

Ultimately, the gospel is the valid and proven truth for our time. So—bad news and good news—the gospel is essential.

Questions for Reflection

- Consider for a moment the way in which you think of the subject of the gospel—when/if you think of it at all. Do you think of the gospel of Jesus Christ as "that sweet story of old"?
- Is it a fairy tale–like story for the benefit of little children and old people?
- Do you ever perceive the gospel of Christ as the explosive power of God for the salvation of the human race?
- As far as you personally are concerned, what is the real meaning of the gospel?
- Let us attempt to be honest here. To what extent do we find ourselves sharing this gospel with others? That is, the whole gospel—the bad news and the good news?
- In other words, are we actually fulfilling the great commission that Christ gave his followers?

Who ... Me?

> As Jesus passed along the Sea of Galilee, he saw Simon and his brother Andrew casting a net into the sea—for they were fishermen. And Jesus said to them, "Follow me and I will make you fish for people." And immediately they left their nets and followed him. As he went a little farther, he saw James son of Zebedee and his brother John, who were in the boat mending their nets. Immediately he called them; and they left their father Zebedee in the boat with the hired men, and followed him. (Mark 1:16–20)

There they are again! Those two compelling words: *Follow me!* There is something mysterious and strange about those words. They always seem to have the power to reach out and touch us on the shoulder. Of course, we know that they were spoken centuries ago in another time and place. That does not, however, erase the fact that they always seem to reach out and tap us on the shoulder. We know that they were originally spoken by a certain man of Galilee to other men of Galilee. Nevertheless, those words, *Follow me,* retain the power to claim our attention. Could it be possible that they are as much intended for us of this time in history as they were for those men in the first century?

It continues the same today. The call of God reaches to the mill, the factory, and the farm. It calls us from the doldrums of mediocrity and the depths of sin, the unexpected and the unsuspecting, and changes his followers. He makes them bearers of the good news of the kingdom of God.

Now for the clincher! God wants you! In this quiet and reflective setting, you sense his divine presence with you. You know he wants you to follow him. You are aware that God is trying to capture your attention. Do not be fearful. Do not hesitate. Just listen. See! He is calling you.

Questions for Reflection

- In your opinion, what is meant by the phrase, "the call of God?"
- Who are the called?
- How about yourself? Are you a follower of Christ?
- Frequently it has been pointed out that the present generation is the generation of the noninvolved. Do you agree? Are you noninvolved in the critical moral and spiritual issues of our time?
- God needs you. He needs you now. Are you listening? How will you respond to God's call to you?
- A word of advice: *follow him.*

Forgiveness

When Jesus saw their faith, he said to the paralytic, "Son, your sins are forgiven." (Mark 2:5; see vs. 1–12)

The first need of every person is forgiveness. Often it is true that our physical ailments are but symptoms of our sin. This likely was the case with the paralytic. Such was the Jesus way of doing things. The truly Christian and sane approach to life is the probe into the deeper sources of evil. One may wonder just how much of our time is wasted foolishly on the symptoms and consequences of sin rather than on the cause itself. In the religious world, we lag miles behind the worlds of science and medicine in our dealing with the evils and ills of our day.

Much attention is given in our time among religious people to the mission of trying to mend broken lives and broken homes. It is essential in this effort that we get to the root cause of the problem. Lives are broken because of sin. Homes are broken because of sin. It is imperative, therefore, that something redemptive is done regarding the matter of sin.

Jesus Christ has delivered the only sure cure for all the world's ills. His cure is the gospel of the kingdom of God which brings conviction of sin, provides forgiveness for sin, and grants the power to overcome sin.

Questions for Reflection

- As a society, do we take the matter of sin seriously?
- Personally, do you take seriously the matter of sin in your own life?
- Have you considered the degree to which the sin in your life affects your daily living?
- Have you in recent times made the effort to catalogue your known sins?
- If so, do you have a desire to be free of them?
- Have you talked this over with God? In other words, have you asked God to forgive you, cleanse you, and guide you in the way of righteousness?
- If not, why not? Right now—this very moment—would be the perfect time to seek and receive the forgiveness of God. He is willing and ready! Are you?

To Those Who Have, More Will Be Given

To those who have, more will be given. (Mark 4:25; see vs. 21-25)

If considered in isolation, this is an excellent proof-text for those persons who insist that life is unfair. After all, they insist, the rich always get richer while the poor get poorer. Then along comes the Holy Bible and its grand declaration: "To those who have, more will be given."

Before we react to this text by applying it to such things as money, property, or worldly position, let us consider a simple question: "What is Jesus talking about?" A careful examination of the larger lesson reveals that Jesus is discussing spiritual matters that pertain to the kingdom of God. With that in mind, what do these words say to us?

Simply stated, we increase in our knowledge and understanding of God, the gospel, and the kingdom of God in direct proportion to the degree to which we devote ourselves to diligent worship, study, and service. In other words, the closer we walk in fellowship with God, the greater the experience of grace, inner strength, and spiritual insight we are granted.

Have you noticed the additional warning? Well, here it is: "From those who have nothing, even what they have will be taken away." The meaning is quite clear! If we fail to respond positively to the kingdom truth we are given, we shall lose God's best for us. Who wants that to happen?

Questions for Reflection

- Are you willing to face your own status in this formula?
- Are you gaining or losing what you have?
- If you desire to be richer in the things of the Lord, how do you propose to accomplish such a goal?
- What about the stewardship of your time?
- Your possessions?
- Your social position in life?
- Ultimately, just how important to you is having "more" of the kingdom's blessings in your life? Are you willing to make the necessary effort?

Signs and Wonders

On that day, when evening had come, he said to them, "Let us go across to the other side." And leaving the crowd behind, they took him with them in the boat, just as he was. Other boats were with him. A great windstorm arose, and the waves beat into the boat, so that the boat was already being swamped. But he was in the stern, asleep on the cushion; and they woke him up and said to him, "Teacher, do you not care that we are perishing?" He woke up and rebuked the wind, and said to the sea, "Peace! Be still." Then the wind ceased, and there was a dead calm. He said to them, "Why are you afraid? Have you still no faith?" And they were filled with great awe and said to one another, "Who then is this, that even the wind and sea obey him?" (Mark 4:35–41)

How great are his signs … (Daniel 4:3)

We will profit greatly if we learn to distinguish between living and life. As a rule, our concept of living retains a certain survival implication. Therefore, we often speak of the necessity of making a living. There is much more to the life of which Jesus spoke than mere living.

Perhaps that is one reason why his miracles were so vital to his ministry. They were signs by which people might ascertain something of the ultimate quality of real life, eternal life, the kind not circumscribed by death.

Miracles are still available today. They occur regularly. Every time the survival notion of an individual is transformed to an awareness of Jesus's kind of life, an authentic miracle has taken place. That is a sign for the rest of us to know that God's kingdom is coming! Indeed, it already is among us.

There is room in the life of every person for the miraculous. It is sad that our generation is so focused upon the technical, objective, and actual that the transcendent, subjective, and essential are squeezed out of our experience. Come on! Let us give God an opportunity to provide signs and wonders in our lives.

Questions for Reflection

- Are you able to identify with the disciples in the boat during the storm?
- Ever wonder if Jesus is on board with you? If he is maybe asleep?
- What are the storms in your life at this time?
- Are you trying to handle your boat by yourself?
- Why not call on the Lord to come to your rescue?

Positive Desires

Then he called the crowd again, and said to them, "Listen to me, all of you, and understand: there is nothing outside a person that by going in can defile, but the things that come out are what defile."

When he had left the crowd and entered the house, his disciples asked him about the parable. He said to them, "Then do you also fail to understand? Do you not see that whatever goes into a person from outside cannot defile, since it enters not the heart but the stomach, and goes out into the sewer?" (Thus he declared all foods clean.) And he said, "It is what comes out of a person that defiles. For it is from within, from the human heart, that evil intentions come: fornication, theft, murder, adultery, avarice, wickedness, deceit, licentiousness, envy, slander, pride, folly. All these evil things come from within, and they defile a person." (Mark 7:14–23)

In the normal flow of life circumstances, most of us tend to justify our attitudes and actions in terms of external factors. For certain, environment is a dominant influence upon each of us. None of us can deny this fact.

In terms of human aspirations and desires, we should strive to achieve a positive perspective. In other words, our wants in life should be directed toward the good and the valid. Accordingly, we must control the influence of our environment upon our attitudes and actions.

Jesus perfectly understood human nature. He emphasized the fact that the desires which emerge from each of us are formed by the nature of our inner being. Therefore, if we find ourselves in subjection to the destructive energy of inordinate desire, we should remember that our God can change the inner being. Truly, the Christian religion is the religion of the heart. Thank God, He can change and rearrange to His own glory our sinful hearts. Then, our attitudes and actions will be pure and redemptive.

Questions for Reflection

- Do you think that chronic negativism is a tragic form of mental illness?
- Do you attempt to monitor the nature of your attitudes?
- What about your actions?
- Then, what about your desires?
- To what extent do you attempt to guide yourself to think and act in a way that cultivates emotional and spiritual wholeness?
- Consider Philippians 4:8: "Finally, beloved, whatever is true, whatever is honorable, whatever is just, whatever is pure, whatever is pleasing, whatever is commendable, if there is any excellence and if there is anything worthy of praise, think about these things."
- Is this passage a worthy pattern for you to follow?

A Lesson in Tolerance

John said to him, "Teacher, we saw someone casting out demons in your name, and we tried to stop him, because he was not following us." But Jesus said, "Do not stop him; for no one who does a deed of power in my name will be able soon afterward to speak evil of me. Whoever is not against us is for us. For truly I tell you, whoever gives you a cup of water to drink because you bear the name of Christ will by no means lose the reward." (Mark 9:38–41)

Notice the words of Jesus: "Whoever is not against us is for us." Christians are perceived by many as being highly intolerant. As a rule, we become so provincial and circumscribed in our doctrinal posturing that we reject any person or group who fails to affirm our point of view. With considerably less objective hostility than exists between the Catholics and Protestants of Northern Ireland, we nevertheless experience great difficulty in retaining an open and easy relationship with Christians of other persuasions than our own.

The issue in this difficult saying of Jesus has nothing to do with which religion is better than another. We could debate that silly matter forever! This saying has to do with the manifestation of the humble awareness of the worth of other persons and other perspectives than our own. Surely we know by now that God is not as small as any one of our limited interpretations of him. Indeed, God is more than all Christian dogmas and all Christian disciplines combined. For any one of us, or any one group of us, to assume that we have a corner on the real and ultimate truth of God is to make a mockery of the very essence of Deity.

Do you suppose that we shall ever arrive at the point where we shall not judge others by some ecclesiastical label but rather by the love, care, and devotion to God and humanity which is in their hearts? May God hasten the day!

Questions for Reflection

- Have you evaluated you own level of tolerance for persons who are not of your particular group?
- Are you able to apply the words of Jesus to your own attitudes and actions?
- If taken seriously, how will these words of Jesus influence your life?
- Try to be honest with yourself: What are some of the ways that your attitudes of intolerance express themselves? Prejudicial comparisons? Jokes which cast a negative view of other persons or denominational groups? The impulse to refute, debate, ignore, or even insult another person?
- Verbal criticism of the liturgy, faith creeds and traditions of other groups are common manifestations of intolerance.

Self-Control

> If any of you put a stumbling block before one of these little ones who believe in me, it would be better for you if a great millstone were hung around your neck and you were thrown into the sea. If your hand causes you to stumble, cut it off; it is better for you to enter life maimed and to have two hands and to go to hell, to the unquenchable fire. And if your foot causes you to stumble, cut it off; it is better to enter life lame than to have two feet and to be thrown into hell. And if your eye causes you to stumble, tear it out; it is better for you to enter the Kingdom of God with one eye and to have two eyes and to be thrown into hell, where their worm never dies, and the fire is never quenched. (Mark 9:42–48)

These are hard sayings of Jesus even for those who claim to believe that all of the Bible must be taken literally. If so, is this an open door to the practice of self-mutilation? Or shall we search for that redemptive principle common to all the teachings of Jesus? Surely we select the latter option.

What is the point Jesus is making? Well, certainly it is not a design for self-mutilation. Of that we may be certain. He is discussing the important matter of self-control which is essential in the life of each Christian. By the use of a literary form known as hyperbole, or overexaggeration, Jesus shocks his hearers into confronting a matter of supreme importance.

In practical terms, self-control makes possible a positive life of meaningful contribution. On the other hand, lack of self-control results in failure and misery in this life and, when taken to extreme, in eternity as well. The point of Jesus is quite specific: Our choice is self-control or self-destruction. One way allows the peace and rest of God, but the other is called hell!

Questions for Reflection

- We have become familiar with many modern maxims which tantalize personal liberty. Some of them you recall:
- "Let it all hang out."
- "If it feels good—do it!"
- "You only go around once."
- "Go for it!"
- Take a few moments and measure these common comments with the sayings of Jesus. Now, how do they fare?
- Focus your reflections on yourself. Who is in charge of you? Candidly, have you mastered self-control?
- Perhaps we have come to realize that we all are in need of the presence of the Spirit of God in our lives. Thereby, he can fulfill the promise of Jesus: he will lead us in the paths of truth and righteousness. Amen.

Redemptive Curiosity

> As he was setting out on a journey, a man ran up and knelt before him, and asked him, "Good Teacher, what must I do to inherit eternal life?" Jesus said to him, "Why do you call me good? No one is good but God alone. You know the commandments: 'You shall not murder; You shall not commit adultery; You shall not steal; You shall not bear false witness; You shall not defraud; Honor your father and mother.'" He said to him, "Teacher, I have kept all these since my youth." Jesus, looking at him, loved him and said, "You lack one thing; go, sell what you own, and give the money to the poor, and you will have treasure in heaven; then come, follow me." When he heard this, he was shocked and went away grieving, for he had many possessions. (Mark 10:17–22)

Each of us is endowed with a purposeful quality which we may call "redemptive curiosity." If we allow ourselves, we will find ourselves in quest of the truth that saves and satisfies. Essentially, we are restless spirits in search of God's quietude. Such is the nature of humankind created as we are in the image of God.

Our ties with the secular and material kingdom often

create barriers to the quest for ultimate spiritual reality available in the spiritual kingdom of God. Jesus was aware of our plight. Hence, his strong counsel: "Come, follow me." In other words, we are to prune away the threatening growth of the secular and material influences and eagerly cultivate our inherent redemptive curiosity. Much is dependent upon our decision in the matter, even our salvation.

Questions for Reflection

- Are you a person who likes to know what is on the other side of the hill?
- Do you become restless when you perceive that you are "living life in a rut"?
- Do you find yourself embracing the idea or reality of change?
- Are you aware that the Christian life is filled with exciting and unexpected adventure—if you really follow Jesus?
- Following Jesus involves a decision to do so. Are you prepared to make such a decision—and mean it?
- Well, he is calling you. Now, it is your move!

Faith in God

In the morning as they passed by, they saw the fig tree withered away to its roots. Then Peter remembered and said to him, "Rabbi, look! The tree that you cursed has withered." Jesus answered them, "Have faith in God. Truly I tell you, if you say to this mountain, 'Be taken up and thrown into the sea,' and if you do not doubt in your heart, but believe that what you say will come to pass, it will be done for you. So I tell you, whatever you ask for in prayer, believing that you have received it, and it will be yours." (Mark 11:20–24)

To have faith in God is to have confidence in God's providence. The past century has witnessed its share of deeds born in the mind of Satan which defy thought of divine providence. For example, we have experienced poison gas, the death march, the concentration camps, racial genocide, and the hydrogen bomb.

This is the age of bottled murder which goes by the title of bonded bourbon. It is the era of hallucinatory high on drugs guaranteed to provide a mental and psychical low. It is the time of the new morality which is nothing more than animal morality.

We are witnesses to the reign of the secular over the

sacred, and the profanation of the holy is the by-product of an increasingly atheistic influence. Is all lost? The response of an authentic faith is *Never!* Listen to the affirmation of faith that Paul sets forth:

> For I am convinced that neither death nor life, nor angels nor principalities, nor things present, nor things to come, nor powers, nor height, nor depth, nor anything else in all creation, will be able to separate us from the love of God in Christ Jesus our Lord. (Romans 8:38–39)

Questions for Reflection

- When thinking seriously and critically regarding our times and circumstances, do you often find yourself questioning the providence of God?
- Do you ever replicate in thought or action the prayer of the disciples: "Help my unbelief"?
- When you realize such thoughts are present, do they give you alarm pertaining to your relationship with God?
- Perhaps there is a formula that may prove helpful to you: Do not surrender your faith to your doubts, but submit your doubts to the power of your faith.
- In all issues of life, depend upon the Word of God; regularly read the Word of God; memorize key portions of the Word of God; quote those key passages in defiance of the threat of your fear, hesitance to trust in God, and the very real influence of those dastardly doubts.

Love – The Great Commandment

> One of the scribes came near and heard them disputing with one another, and seeing that he answered them well, he asked him, "Which commandment is the first of all?" Jesus answered, "The first is 'Hear O Israel: The Lord our God, the Lord is one; you shall love the Lord your God with all your heart, and with all your soul, and with all your mind, and with all your strength.' The second is this, 'You shall love your neighbor as yourself.' There is no other commandment greater than these."
> (Mark 12:28–31)

The notion of Christian love seems to be a grand and achievable objective. One wonders, therefore, why authentic love is often difficult to actualize. As strange as it may seem, at first glance, the word *prejudice* may play a role in the process. The word *prejudice* has a very narrow connotation as a rule. All too often we have limited the word to the idea of racial discrimination. However, the word has far broader implications.

A person can be prejudiced against an art form. Because of the environment in which one grew up where great music was not the norm, there can exist the feeling that a classical concert would have limited value. This is prejudice of the highest order. It is prejudice born of ignorance.

In the same sense, we are all quite familiar with the ugly prejudice that often exists even in the Christian community itself. One denomination can be prejudiced against another, and yet both groups think of themselves as "Christian." In this regard, it becomes clear how prejudice can exist as a barrier against Christian love.

Clearly, the Christian faith, which is based on "God so loved the world," is a challenge for each and all of us to rid ourselves of our prejudice and love, truly love everybody. Of course, it will be difficult to do. But surely it will be worth the doing.

Questions for Reflection

- Is it possible to love a person or group without liking the person or group?

- Sometimes self-analysis is of significant value. Therefore, make a list of five persons whom you do not like:

- Now, make a list of five reasons why you should make a real effort to like those persons:

- One more list! List five ways you may begin developing an authentic love for those persons.

PART THREE

THE GOSPEL OF
LUKE

Jesus: God and Man?

The angel said to her, "Do not be afraid, Mary, for you have found favor with God. And now you will conceive in your womb and bear a son, and you will name him Jesus. He will be great, and will be called the Son of the Most High, and the Lord God will give him the throne of his ancestor, David. He will reign over the house of Jacob forever, and of his kingdom there will be no end." Mary said to the angel, "How can this be, since I am a virgin?" The angel said to her, "The Holy Spirit will come upon you, and the power of the Most High will overshadow you; therefore the child to be born will be holy; he will be called the Son of God." (Luke 1:30–35)

Something about the birth of Jesus is incredible if the premise is accepted that Jesus is divine. After all, Jesus was born in the identical manner of all other babies. The Bible is quite clear in that regard. So what are we to make of this?

The whole matter of Jesus's life on earth becomes absurd unless we accept the fact that the life of Jesus was truly a human life. We are taught in the Bible that Jesus was first a baby, then a boy, then a man. The life of Jesus was in the truest sense the life of a man. How, then, was he different from us?

Jesus was different from us in that he did not yield to our common temptations. He won the battle against sin. Accordingly, the apostle Paul may say that we "shall be saved by his life" (Romans 5:10 KJV). Amen! And by his death and resurrection which inherently are a part of his life.

Questions for Reflection

- Are you able to comprehend and embrace the concept of any person being God/man?
- When adding the name *Jesus* to the mix, how does that simplify the issue?
- Honestly, is this idea difficult for you to assimilate into your own reason construct?
- How could we ever understand anything about God if he had not incarnated himself into human terms?

Good News for You

> In that region there were shepherds living in the fields, keeping watch over their flocks by night. Then an angel of the Lord stood before them, and the glory of the Lord shone around them, and they were terrified. But the angel said to them, "Do not be afraid; for see—I am bringing you good news of great joy for all the people: to you is born this day in the city of David a Savior, who is the Messiah, the Lord." (Luke 2:8–11)

These familiar and greatly loved words are the nucleus of the angel's message on the first Christmas to the humble shepherds of the Judean hills. It is interesting that the angels made their announcement to shepherds and not to the rulers or the wealthy or even the religious leaders. But then, why not the shepherds? After all, they were representative of the best sort of Jew. They were not the socially elite of the day, but they were spiritual and they were devout in their faith in the Lord of the holy Scriptures. About the shepherds, we may detect their wonder and awe that God is active in behalf of mankind.

Pointed implications may be drawn from the event and applied to our own generation. In the first place, it is God who takes the initiative on man's behalf. The revelation of the advent of Jesus came to the shepherds from heaven. They had not gone in search of it. Second, salvation is not class-conscious but is obviously amenable to those whose attitude is conditioned by genuine piety and an active faith in the God who acts. Then, the experience with God is best realized in the atmosphere of wonder, reverence, and worship. That constitutes the best counsel for us who would seek for true meaning in the Advent celebration. There is the secret: wonder, reverence, and worship.

Questions for Reflection

- Did you take note of those three important words?
- Wonder! Linger in your thinking about the transcendent mystery involved in Deity becoming human. This remains the singular event in the human journey that remains utterly indescribable.
- Reverence! The mere contemplation of that glorious event motivates the human spirit to bow in adoration, prayer, and humility.
- Worship! This is the time for the choirs and the triumphant notes of Handel's "Hallelujah" chorus. Indeed, God is near; let all the earth praise his name.
- Perhaps the song of the angels is perfect for this moment:

    > Glory to God in the highest heaven, and
    > on earth peace among those whom he
    > favors! (2:14)

To Make Christ Known

When he came to Nazareth, where he had been brought up, he went to the synagogue on the sabbath day, as was his custom. He stood up to read, and the scroll of the prophet Isaiah was given to him. He unrolled the scroll and found the place where it was written:

"The Spirit of the Lord is upon me,
    because he has anointed me
        to bring good news to the poor.
He has sent me to proclaim release to the captives
    and recovery of sight to the blind,
        to let the oppressed go free,
to proclaim the year of the Lord's favor." (Luke 4:16–19)

Jesus declared, "The Spirit of the Lord is upon me, because he has anointed me to preach the good news to the poor." It is obvious that this was at least a part of the ministry of Jesus. But several questions come to mind regarding the preaching of the gospel. Is every Christian involved in the ministry? What does it really mean to "preach" the gospel? What is the gospel?

The word *ministry* can properly denote the function of those who serve the church in set-apart positions. But there is the ministry of the whole people of God, i.e., the church as a whole. The Christian ministry should be understood more in terms of function rather than of office or status. The term *ministry* has its basis in the word *minister* and means servant, attendant, minister, or deacon.

In this passage, the phrase "preach the good news" is especially significant. Two observations may be made: (1) The phrase refers to the good news of Jesus Christ. (2) The verb is used of any message designed primarily to cheer the hearers. Clearly, each Christian is in the ministry of sharing the good news of Jesus Christ with others. In its finest sense, to preach the gospel is to make Christ known. All Christians are commissioned to make Christ known.

Questions for Reflection

- Do you usually think of "minister" in terms of a professional functionary?
- Does such thinking create the illusion of an elite group of people who are somewhat exclusive in nature?
- If embraced as valid, does this notion give a pass to "regular" Christians? In other words, do we sometimes think that the professional ministers are the ones paid to do the job?
- Are you beginning to understand that you are in ministry yourself?
- In what ways are you responding to your assigned task?

A Strange Paradox

> After this, he went out and saw a tax collector named Levi, sitting at the tax-booth; and he said to him, "Follow me." And he got up, left everything, and followed him.
>
> Then Levi gave a great banquet for him in his house; and there was a large crowd of tax collectors and others sitting at the table with them. The Pharisees and the scribes were complaining to his disciples, saying, "Why do you eat and drink with tax collectors and sinners?" Jesus answered, "Those who are well have no need of a physician, but those who are sick; I have come to call not the righteous but sinners to repentance." (Luke 5:27–32)

It seems that a major interest of the adult generation is to shield the youth from exposure to evil company and bad influence. To accommodate this purpose, many mottos and slogans have been developed. One such gem of wisdom goes like this: "If you lie down with dogs, you will get up with fleas."

The main idea is that good people seek the company of good people in order that they may stay good people. Then along comes Jesus with one of his revolutionary observations. The sinless Christ declared that the object of his ministry was to bring sinners to himself. That is an amazing paradox.

Just imagine! The spotless and sinless hands of Jesus are extended to the sinner. The soil you will find on the Savior is not his soil; it is the dirt of us sinners. Does the idea begin to get through to you that you are precious in the sight of the Lord? God sees you as a sinner and loves you in spite of what you are and because of what you can become. Therefore, he calls you to come to him in repentance and faith.

Questions for Reflection

- Do you ever feel like crying out, "Jesus, what have I to do with you?"
- After all, if Jesus is God and I am sinner, then what do we have in common?
- Consider this: We do have something in common—that is, love!
- God loves us, and therefore, we are able to love God.
- The paradox becomes even more stark. How can God hate sin and still love the sinner?

To Whom Little Is Forgiven

Therefore, I tell you, her sins, which were many, have been forgiven; hence she has shown great love. But the one to whom little is forgiven, loves little. Luke 7:47 (see vs. 36–50)

It is strange that we Christians frequently are without emotion when thinking, talking, or singing about our relationship with the Lord. How can this be?

Is it possible that we tend to view ourselves as basically good people? Bad people are murderers, prostitutes, rapists, and suchlike. We certainly are not any of the above. Whatever sins we may commit do not qualify as being really bad. Do they? So when God forgives us, he does not have as much to forgive as in the case of those bad sinners.

Maybe we have discovered the reason for some of our shallow and lackluster religious commitment. In contrast, it will be helpful to reflect on the way God views sin and sinners. In the eyes of God, human sin is not so much a breaking of social and moral codes as it an action or attitude against God himself. Therefore, our socially acceptable "mistakes" are as blatant sins against God as are the flagrant transgressions of those "bad sinners." If this ever sinks in as being the truth, we shall have great cause to rejoice that God has forgiven us.

Questions for Reflection

- Are you willing and able to look honestly at yourself?
- How do you view your relationship with God?
- Are you as judicious regarding your personal shortcomings as you are about the shortcomings of others?
- How excited are you when you think about your sins being forgiven?
- Like the forgiven woman, can you now show great love?

Radical Discipleship

> Let the dead bury their own dead; but as for you, go and proclaim the kingdom of God .... No one who puts his hand to the plow and looks back is fit for the kingdom of God. (Luke 9:60, 62; see vs. 57–62)

It is especially true in the United States that being a Christian is not a costly process in terms of lost status, lost fortune, and lost life. Such has not always been the case. The threat to authentic discipleship in our culture is far more subjective and subtle than in former years. Presumed social and domestic relationships and responsibilities form a surprising barrier to genuine commitment to Christ and his kingdom.

Again, we are confronted with the question of taking literally the words of Jesus in this passage of rather harsh and cold directives. We know that Jesus never abrogated the significance of the family. He loved his own mother and even honored her needs while dying on the cross. What, therefore, is the principle emerging from this difficult passage that will give guidance to us today?

The service of Jesus must never be entered into casually. While family relationships, the exacting of a livelihood, and fulfilling important social duties are normal for the Christian, nothing—absolutely nothing—is to take precedence over the primacy of loyalty and service to the Master. Following Jesus is a joyful experience, but it also is a demanding one. Let us never ignore that fact.

Questions for Reflection

- What is the most important thing in your life?
- Who is the most important person in your life?
- To what or to whom do you give the majority of your time? Your energy? Your financial resources?
- In other words, what or who is your God?
- When thinking about your financial securities, your property, and even your family, to what extent are you prepared to leave all and follow Jesus?
- To state it another way, what does being a true disciple of Jesus Christ mean to you?

The Imperative of Love

> Just then a lawyer stood up to test Jesus. "Teacher," he said, "What must I do to inherit eternal life?" He answered, "What do you read there?" He answered, "You shall love the Lord your God with all your heart, and with all your soul, and with all your strength, and with all your mind; and your neighbor as yourself." And Jesus said to him, "You have given the right answer; do this and you will live." (Luke 10:25–28)

Jesus declared that the greatest of all commands is to love God with all of one's being, and to love one's neighbor as oneself. That is correct, for he made the two laws one. We have a problem here because of the relationship between commandment and love. Can one be required to love? Is there an imperative mood of the verb *love*?

The New Testament idea of love is radically different from our contemporary idea. For Jesus and the apostles, *love* was not so much an emotional word as it was an action word. Thus, it is clear how we may be commanded to "love our neighbor." Christian social love becomes actualized. We recognize the presence of other people besides ourselves in the world. We consider their interests as well as our own. We genuinely care for their health and prosperity. We move from the selfish "live and let live" attitude to the Christian view of "live and help live." Such satisfies the imperative of love in the New Testament sense.

Questions for Reflection

- What is the difference between the "love" of which Jesus spoke and any other kind?
- Is the Jesus kind of "love" practical in our time?
- Are you able to distinguish between the different kinds of love which you experience in your own life?
- Can you think of someone whom you know you do not love?
- Would Jesus think of them as your neighbor? Do you?
- In light of these reflections, what are you going to do about your relationship with the person whom you do not love?

Understanding Life

> Then he told them a parable: "The land of a rich man produced abundantly. And he thought to himself, 'What should I do, for I have no place to store my crops?' Then he said, 'I will do this: 'I will pull down my barns and build larger ones, and there I will store all my grain and my goods. And I will say to my soul, 'Soul, you have ample goods laid up for many years; relax, eat, drink, and be merry.' But God said to him, 'You fool! This very night your life is being demanded of you. And the things you have prepared, whose will they be?' So it is with those who store up treasures for themselves but are not rich toward God." (Luke 12:16–21)

"What are you living for?" Sadly, far too many of us never face that question because it is too intimidating. After all, we are so busy accumulating the conveniences and luxuries with which to live that we have little time to reflect on life's goal—what we are living for. So today, let us consider the supreme importance of having an appropriate goal in life. After all, what does it matter if we have everything with which to live, and nothing for which to live?

There may never have been a generation more dramatically caught in the tension between the things with which to live and the goals to live for than our own. And let us face it honestly: the things with which to live are very desirable. Without doubt, they are the marketable commodities of our time. They sparkle! They are alluring, seductive, and compelling. Most of us are excessively vulnerable to them.

Yet, there remains a certain unsettled feeling about us all. There are those strange whisperings in the dark that provoke us to think more deeply about the meaning of life and our own unique destiny. Could it be that Jesus was correct when he observed, "A man's life does not consist of the abundance of the things which he possesses" (Luke 12:15)?

Questions for Reflection

- Are you sensitive to the teachings of Jesus regarding materialism?
- To what extent have you allowed yourself to be seduced into the race for "the things of earth"?
- Do the "things" of your life really provide you with happiness—permanently?
- Do you have the will and ability to change your lifestyle?
- Prayerfully consider the familiar lines from this beloved song:

Turn your eyes upon Jesus,
Look full in His wonderful face,

And the things of earth will grow strangely dim
In the light of His glory and grace.

Little Is Big When God Is in It

> He said therefore, "What is the kingdom of God like? And to what should I compare it? It is like a mustard seed that someone took and sowed in the ground; it grew and became a tree, and the birds of the air made nests in its branches." (Luke 13:18–19)

One may wonder how much of today's anxiety is due in large measure to our compulsion to keep pace? There is ample evidence that such is the case. From the compulsive acquisition of the nonessential kitchen gadget to the instillation in our double garage of the superfluous advanced design automobile, we, as a society, operate on the premise that the quantity of life is the primary goal of life. Thus, we have become the generation that has everything with which to live, but little for which to live.

Surely most of us will agree that it is the natural inclination of human nature to give special favor to the big. Therefore, when you look at the parable of the mustard seed, you are surprised at its radical antisocial emphasis. Actually, it declares that little is big when God is in it. This is one way of pointing out the fallacy of the quantity syndrome. To state it plainly, to confuse size with significance is the ultimate vulgarity. This is a difficult lesson for us when our entire orientation is toward the worship of the bulk. Thus, we shall do well to avoid thinking that bigger is better.

Questions for Reflection

- Do you find that this discussion challenges your approach to life?
- For example, to be very personal, what factors determined the choice you made in becoming a member of your church?
- Did size of membership, budget, or nature of the program provided determine your decision?
- Speaking of reasons for choices, what about your house or your car?
- How does Jesus's parable of the mustard seed apply to your own life?

Invitation to Life

> At the time for the dinner he sent his servant to say to those who had been invited, "Come; for everything is ready now." (Luke 14:17; see vs. 15–24)

Christianity should be comparable to a great celebration. There is every evidence that Christ intended that authentic religion should epitomize joy and happiness. Surely we know that there exists a great need for celebration in today's society

To portray the Christian religion as a gloomy existence is to deny its very nature as taught in the New Testament and experienced by millions of devoted Christians past and present. To embrace the Christian faith does not involve giving up laughter and sunshine. To embrace the Christian faith is to enter a happy fellowship with life, with other people, and with God. To embrace the Christian religion is to experience a kind of joy that never can be realized in any other sphere of human relationships.

Thus, it is the responsibility of Christians to perpetually voice God's invitation to all persons at all times. Ours is an invitation to embrace the joy of life. The invitation is general, because everyone is invited. It is personal, because each person is invited. You cannot answer for anyone else. Will you embrace the joy?

Questions for Reflection

- Have you given serious thought to the reality of being a recipient of an invitation from God himself?
- Do you feel that you are experiencing the abundant life?
- What about that exuberant joy promised you?
- Perhaps you realize that it now is your time to respond to God's invitation and enter that abundant life.

On Being Yourself

> But when he came to himself he said, "How many of my father's hired hands have bread enough and to spare, but here I am dying of hunger! I will get up and go to my father, and I will say to him, 'Father, I sinned against heaven and before you; I am no longer worthy to be called your son; treat me like one of your hired hands.'" (Luke 15:17–19; see vs. 11–24)

Surely the ultimate goal of each of us is to become the person God intended us to be. In other words, "Be yourself" is sound advice.

Frequently, in the pursuit of this goal, we are confronted with the task of making the best of adverse circumstances, and refusing to allow them to make the worst of us.

> Fate slew him but he did not drop;
> She felled—he did not fall—
> Impaled him on her fiercest stakes—
> He neutralized them all.
>
> —Anon.

Recall the most incisive and provocative phrase of Jesus's parable of the prodigal son: "When he came to himself." The young man's road to renewal began right there. Truly,

Christian conversion is realized when any person submits to God to become the person he was created to be.

Questions for Reflection

- Consider the counsel of Socrates (and of Polonius): "Know thyself." Do you know yourself?
- Take a few minutes and write answers to the following familiar questions: Who am I? Why am I here? Where am I going?
- Are you happy in your present state of life? If not, why not?
- Have you attempted any remedies to correct the present unhappy aspects of your life?
- Have you given God's simple formula a chance? And what is that formula? Just this: (1) Look at yourself. (2) Trust in God. (3) Take action on your own behalf.
- One more glance at our key text: "I will arise and go to my father!" If it worked then, why not now with you?

Authentic Humility

> Who among you would say to your servant who has just come in from plowing or tending sheep in the field, "Come here at once and take your place at the table?" Would you not rather say to him, "Prepare supper for me, put on your apron and serve me while I eat and drink; later you may eat and drink"? Do you thank the servant for doing what was commanded? So you also when you have done all that you were ordered to do, say, "We are worthless servants; we have done only what we ought to have done." (Luke 17:7–10)

We all speak from time to time of humility. However, have you noticed that the world is not flooded with people volunteering to be humble? It may be that we do not understand the true meaning of humility.

If by humility we mean the character quality found in the unctuous, bland, self-depreciating person who makes us feel squirmy and uncomfortable, then forget it! Who wants to be that kind of humble person?

However, the humility of the gracious-minded person who possesses the capacity of authentic acceptance, both of himself and others, provides us with a desirable option. Here one thinks of the "grace of humility" and feels a genuine desire to experience it.

So the unworthy servant manifests true humility, the kind born of the grace of God, nurtured by the love of God, and affirmed by the Spirit of God.

Questions for Reflection

- Are you acquainted with anyone who you believe is truly humble?
- What is there about that person that you admire and desire to be true of yourself?
- Is that person aware of the presence of those desirable characteristics within him/her?
- What are you doing to develop such qualities in your own life?

The Way to Perfect Health

> Then Jesus said, "Father, forgive them; for they do not know what they are doing." (Luke 23:34; see vs. 32–38)

Has it ever occurred to you that Jesus was never sick? If he was, there is no record of it. No colds, no fevers, no heart trouble, no ulcers, no strokes. Think of it! How did he pull it off? It may be that the spirit of forgiveness so bathed his heart and mind of all particles of resentment that love and tenderness totally filled him. This was the basis for his health. No wonder he was never sick.

We have come to an unexplored region of the redemptive process. The kind of forgiveness for which Jesus prayed was the ultimate redemption of humanity from sick minds, sick bodies, and sick souls. He realized that spiritually healthy persons never murder others on a cross. Hence his admonition, "They do not know what they do." When sinners are really forgiven and accept the benefits contingent with the experience of forgiveness, happiness and peace exist to become reality, not idealistic fantasies. Forgiveness cleanses the human heart and assures health.

Jesus prayed, "Father, forgive them; for they do not know what they are doing." May his prayer be answered this day—in us.

Questions for Reflection

- This is a tough one! Do you carry grudges?
- Is it difficult to "forgive and forget"?
- Do you sense tension and anxiety when encountering a person who you believe has hurt you?
- How can you experience psychological and spiritual health and wholeness until you are liberated from the negative influence of such past experiences?
- Jesus has given us the perfect prescription for real health: "When you pray, say … forgive us *as* we forgive" (see Luke 11:2–4).

The Great Promise

He replied, "Truly I tell you, today you will be with me in Paradise." (Luke 23:43; see vs. 39–43)

The future of Jesus and the future of humanity are closely related in our text. Jesus told the dying criminal that they would both be together in Paradise. The word *paradise* is a Persian word and means "walled garden." In ancient times, when a Persian king desired to especially reward one of his subjects, he did so by making a companion of him and walking with him in the garden. Thus, the thief was promised more than immortality; he was assured of fellowship with Christ in the garden of heaven.

Yet, while the future nature of heaven is explicit in the word itself, there seems to be a special connotation here. "Today!" The immediate nature of that word, *today*, captures the attention. In some way, heaven is not to be viewed as some far-off tomorrow, but today; not some prize of a future age to come, but Paradise regained—*now*! The point is that where Jesus is, there is heaven. Press that idea one step further: If Jesus really lives within your life, if you are a "fleshed-out Christ," it may be that heaven is where you are.

Questions for Reflection

- Is life for you more like heaven or hell?
- Relate your present situation in life with the promise of Jesus: "Today, you will be with me in Paradise."
- Does it fit?
- How about the notion that if Jesus lives in your life, then heaven is where you are?
- Do you think that those persons closest to you would agree?

The Gauntlet of the Galilean

> Thus it is written, that the Messiah is to suffer and to rise from the dead on the third day, and that repentance and forgiveness of sins is to be proclaimed in his name to all nations, beginning from Jerusalem. (Luke 24:46–47)

Frequently we Christians become immersed in discussions regarding the central task of the church. To state it differently, what is our priority emphasis in Christ's church? It is the opinion of some that one particular emphasis should be dominant, while others believe that another emphasis should take precedence. What is taught in the Bible?

To the surprise of many, it is impossible to find in the sacred scriptures many of the programs and activities that occupy so much of our time, energy, and finances in today's organized religious life. Throughout the Bible the central focus is fixed on the divine purpose of God's mission to the world. Specifically, that purpose remains the preaching of the gospel of Jesus Christ to all the nations.

The Galilean cast his gauntlet in our path with his ringing call, "Follow me." Then followed his clear command: "Go ye …." Any further debate regarding the central task of the church is but "sound and fury, signifying nothing." Jesus's word is the last word, and his word is pronounced "Mission."

Questions for Reflection

- Is the structure and mission of the modern church anything close to the New Testament pattern?
- What is the responsibility of the Christian to influence the contemporary church toward the biblical pattern?
- Do you think the "true church" exists in today's world?
- If so, identify and describe it.
- In your judgment, in what ways do the fragmented segments of modern denominationalism reflect the true church of Jesus Christ?
- Jesus promised that he would "upon this rock ... build [his] church." Does it presently exist? Is it still in process of becoming? And ultimately, is the church as it exists faithfully addressing its central mission of preaching the gospel to all the nations?

PART FOUR

THE GOSPEL OF
JOHN

Tomorrow's Christian

> The true light, which enlightens everyone, was coming into the world.
> He was in the world, and the world came into being through him; yet the world did not know him. He came to what was his own, and his own people did not accept him. But to all who received him, who believed in his name, he gave power to become children of God. (John 1:9–13)

Many contemporary Christians are institution and tradition oriented. Far too many of us are hindered by those seven deadly words, "We never did it that way before." It's too bad that change is the challenge that we dare not accept.

Such is not the case in the world of commerce and industry. In that arena, one may discover an exciting trend: there is increasing emphasis on enabling people to grow and change.

Come to think of it, that always has been the emphasis of Jesus. His ministry, message, and method were universally person-oriented. Consider that he made no overt attempt to change the institution of the Temple or to restructure the priesthood. He merely spent his time responding to people and their needs. But his was a redemptive ministry.

God grant that tomorrow's Christian will serve God in greater harmony with the ministry style of Jesus. Surely that will occur, and, in the process, the Holy Spirit will operate through Christians, transforming and opening them to one another and to God. Better yet, let us so commit our lives to God that we can become tomorrow's Christians today.

Questions for Reflection

- To what extent are you a past-oriented Christian?
- Do traditions dominate your lifestyle?
- Are you able to appropriate and apply these words: "forgetting what lies behind and striving forward to what lies ahead, I press on toward the goal for the prize of the upward call of God in Christ Jesus" (Philippians 3:13–14)?

How to See God

And the Word became flesh and lived among us, and we have seen his glory, the glory as of a father's only son, full of grace and truth …. From his fullness we have all received, grace upon grace. The law indeed was given through Moses; grace and truth came through Jesus Christ. No one has ever seen God. It is God the only Son, who is close to the Father's heart, who has made him known. (John 1:14, 16–18)

It frequently is true that the reality of God is such a problem to some of us that we never achieve that saving relationship with him which is essential for our salvation. After all, we admit that God is the supreme mystery. All our efforts to understand God through prayers, meditations, and logic serve only to intensify the mystery.

When, however, our attention is brought to focus on Jesus Christ, we observe how he spoke of God, spoke to God, and assisted others to believe in God as he believed in God. Inevitably, we reach the conclusion that in Jesus we are seeing God as he really is. In other words, Jesus is not so much the man who comes from God as he is the God who comes for man.

Questions for Reflection

- When you think deeply regarding your relationship with God, how well do you really know him?
- How well do you really know God's Son?
- Does it begin to register with you that the better you know Jesus, the better you know God?
- Are you able to assimilate the reality that to know Jesus is to know God? Do you really understand that Father and Son are really One?

Discipleship: Mystery and Goal

The next day John again was standing with two of his disciples, and as he watched Jesus walked by, he exclaimed, "Look, here is the Lamb of God!" The two disciples heard him say this, and they followed Jesus. When Jesus turned and saw them following, he said to them, "What are you looking for?" They said to him, "Rabbi" (which translated means Teacher), "where are you staying?" He said to them, "Come and see." They came and saw where he was staying, and they remained with him that day. It was about four o'clock in the afternoon. One of the two who heard John speak and followed him was Andrew, Simon Peter's brother. He first found his brother, Simon, and said to him, "We have found the Messiah" (which is translated Anointed). He brought Simon to Jesus, who looking at him said, "You are Simon son of John. You are to be called Cephas" (which is translated Peter). (John 1:35–42)

The mystery of discipleship is a two-way matter. God calls us because he is God and has the authority to do as he wills. But the discipleship process continues only so far as our single-minded obedience extends. Either we belong to God and his purpose for us, or we do not. The issue is that elementary. So, to whom do you belong? God or yourself?

The goal of discipleship is service. Christian discipleship is not a personal fancy, but it is the commission of God. Whatever form the commission of God takes in anyone's life, the mission is always the same. The disciple is the herald of the King, going forth to proclaim the good news of the salvation of God in Jesus Christ. Disciples speak not for themselves but for their King! That sense of belonging to the Lord always results in deep commitment to Christ and service for him.

Questions for Reflection

- Does the idea of a divine commission for you overwhelm you?
- Do you shrink from the thought of some kind of "special service"?
- Do you think the notion of discipleship should be reserved for the professional minister?
- Have you considered talking to God regarding this issue?
- Determine to remain sensitive to the reality of God's presence in your own life. Keep alert! After all, God may be speaking to you.

God's Grace in Action

> For God so loved the world that he gave his only Son, so that everyone who believes in him may not perish but have eternal life.
>
> Indeed, God did not send the Son into the world to condemn the world, but in order that the world might be saved through him. (John 3:16–17)

A personal benefit of Christ's passion is the increasing certainty of personal worth before the Lord. Always Jesus possessed the capacity to recognize the diamond in the rough. He saw in the burly fisherman, Simon, the brilliant Peter of Pentecost.

It is reported that Michelangelo once visited a builder's yard and saw there a stained and altogether unattractive lump of marble. Turning to the attendant, he said, "Take that lump of marble to my studio. There is an angel imprisoned there, and I can set it free."

That is what Jesus can do for you. Your life may seem to yourself and others a misshapen and worthless lump. But Jesus sees in you an angel, and he desires to set you free. He did just that for a certain little Jewish murderer on the road to Damascus. He encountered Saul of Tarsus even when the latter was on the way to kill yet other Christians, and he cut away the hatred and bitterness of the years. As those stained splinters of religious prejudice fell away, the beautiful St. Paul was released to bless all future generations with his message of God's redeeming grace. If Jesus could do that for Saul of Tarsus, he can do it for you as well.

Questions for Reflection

- Do you like yourself as you are?
- Are there times when you are afflicted with feelings of insecurity, inadequacy, inferiority, or less than lovely to look upon?
- When and if assailed with such contemplations, do you ever stop to recall that you are an unfinished symphony, that God continues to develop the harmony of your life?
- Are you aware that God has plans for you and with you that are greater than you are able to imagine?
- Are you able and willing to trust yourself to the hands of God?

The Life of Jesus in the Life of the Believer

> He must increase, but I must decrease .... Whoever believes in the Son has eternal life; whoever disobeys the Son will not see life, but must endure God's wrath. (John 3:30, 36; see vs. 25–36)

What really makes us happy? More money? More friends? More possessions? More status? As a rule, we think of personal happiness in terms of personal appropriation, growth, or expansion. If taken seriously, the words of John the Baptist shatter such reasoning.

> Therefore this joy of mine is now full.
> He must increase, but I must decrease. (John 3:29–30 RSV)

Because of the greatness of Christ, it was the joy of John the Baptist to defer to him. Far too many of us are concerned that we receive full credit for the sake of our own image and ego. We need to realize that we achieve true and lasting happiness only as we place the primary focus of our attention on Christ. Let us speedily learn to accomplish our task and then retreat from the spotlight. As it is written, "To God be the glory."

Questions for Reflection

- How can a person realize true happiness in a world filled with pain and misery?
- Does it help you to remember that the Christian's life has its focus on Jesus Christ?
- Consider that authentic joy is not environmental, but it is spiritual in nature.
- Conclude these reflections for today by reading and reflecting on Philippians 4:4–9.

All Is Not Lost

> Jesus said to her, "Everyone who drinks of this water will be thirsty again, but those who drink of the water that I will give them will never be thirsty. The water that I will give them will become in them a spring of water gushing up into eternal life." (John 4:13–14; see vs. 1–26)

Never has there been a society as saturated in religion, especially the Christian religion, as our own. Yet there exists abundant evidence of hostility to the simple evangelism of New Testament Christianity. Just examine our society for a moment. Notice the extent of disappointment and disillusionment that prevails. Mark the frustration and anxiety under which many of us stagger. Note the extent to which cynicism and despair have taken possession of human souls. For many of us, nothing seems to matter anymore. Those cherished virtues of honesty, chastity, sobriety, and courtesy have become increasingly irrelevant in our secular-oriented society. We have come to a day in which none of us expects anything positive to happen. To couch it in evangelical terms, we are lost! Nevertheless, all is not lost. When the essential energy of the gospel is released, it possesses the power to effectively redeem both the individual and society.

Here is an interesting verse: "For the Son of man came to seek and to save the lost" (Luke 19:10 RSV). It will prove instructive to think about what is lost. Usually, we interpret this text with emphasis on *who* is lost. Make it very personal. In your own life, what is missing? Joy? Peace? Hope? Fellowship? It is the good news of the gospel that God saves not only you, but that which is yours as well. Indeed, because of Jesus, all is not lost.

Questions for Reflection

- Taking stock: Are you as happy today as you were one year ago?
- Are you as happy as you would like to be?
- Do you think that Christ really has made a difference in human history?
- Do you believe that Christ can make a difference in your own personal history?
- Are you willing to permit him to make that difference?
- Would this be a good time for you seriously to invite Christ to take control and guide your mind and heart so that your actions will reflect his presence in your life?

True Worship

> But the hour is coming, and is now here, when the true worshipers will worship the Father in spirit and in truth, for the Father seeks such as these to worship him. God is spirit, and those who worship him must worship him in spirit and truth. (John 4:23–24; see vs. 7–38)

True worship begins with God, and has God as its object. Here is one of the most profound statements regarding the nature of worship to be found anywhere in the Holy Scriptures. It is evident from this important text that in the matter of worship, God is both the subject and the object.

In much of our modern worship, the experience is structured with the worship participants in mind rather than God. It is popular for Christians to talk of attending worship "where I can get something out of it." Such a motivation is misguided and selfish. The central question remains: "What does God receive from our worship?"

There is a beneficial "fallout" for the participant who engages in true worship. When one directs his worship toward God, the experience is spiritually redemptive in that it lifts the worshiper ever nearer to God, the Object of the whole process.

Questions for Reflection

- To what extent is worship truly an essential component of the believer's life?
- In your own personal life, is the practice of prayer a perfunctory exercise in the preservation of tradition?
- Are you able to be honest with yourself? If so, why do you worship?
- Read from Psalm 95:6–7 and discuss its true meaning: "O come, let us worship and bow down, let us kneel before the Lord, our Maker! For he is our God, and we are the people of his pasture, and the sheep of his hand."

On the Desire of the Heart

After this there was a festival of the Jews, and Jesus went up to Jerusalem.

Now in Jerusalem by the Sheep Gate there is a pool, called in Hebrew Beth-zatha, which has five porticoes. In these lay many invalids—blind, lame, and paralyzed. One man was there who had been ill for thirty-eight years. When Jesus saw him lying there and knew that he had been there a long time, he said to him, "Do you want to be made well?" The sick man answered him, "Sir, I have no one to put me into the pool when the water is stirred up; and while I am making my way, someone else steps down ahead of me." Jesus said to him, "Stand up, take your mat and walk." At once the man was made well, and he took up his mat and began to walk. (John 5:1–9)

If it is your desire to be a true Christian, do not delay in the pursuit of your purpose. Do not make the mistake of speculating on alternative life options. Nothing could be a greater tragedy. Press on with your heart and soul until you realize the goal of your desire.

It is the certain promise of Jesus that newness of life and being is available to those persons who seek him with all their hearts. Quality of life is not withheld from anyone. Circumstance of life is not uniform, but neither is it the determining factor. Everything worthy depends on the intensity of desire.

Jesus put it accordingly: *"Do you want to be made well?"* Obviously, the choice is up to you.

Questions for Reflection

- Recall the familiar maxim: "If you want something with all your heart, you will receive it." Do you believe this to be true?
- In light of such thinking, just how serious are you in your desire to achieve a deeper and more meaningful relationship with God?
- At this time in your life, do you have such a relationship?
- Remember the basic lesson of our text: It is up to you!

Jesus: The Bread of Life

> Jesus said to them, "I am the bread of life. Whoever comes to me will never be hungry, and whoever believes in me will never be thirsty." (John 6:35; see vs. 35–40)

When Christ is received into a person's life, his divine nature is so assimilated into the receiving person that soon it is the very life of Christ coursing through his veins. Such is the view of the apostle Paul:

> It is no longer I who live, but Christ lives in me; and the life which I now live in the flesh I live by faith in the Son of God, who loved me and delivered himself for me. (Galatians 2:20)

At the very core of this statement there exists the conviction that Christ is the essential ingredient to realize a full and meaningful life. When Jesus said, "I am the Bread of Life," he was affirming that God has provided for the basic need of each of us. This is the antithesis of the dogma of self-sufficiency. Without the reception of Christ within one's life, there never can be true fulfillment.

Look again at our text, for it portrays the nature of the redemptive process:

Jesus said unto them, "I am the Bread of Life. He who comes to me shall never hunger, and he who believes in me shall never thirst."

Questions for Reflection

- Why does Jesus refer to himself as bread?
- Are you willing to appropriate this image and apply it to your own life? If so, at least two questions are fitting:
- Have you come to Jesus for that living bread?
- Exactly what is it in your life for which you hunger in true sincerity?
- You may be assured that you will be filled and satisfied by a personal encounter with Jesus Christ.

Cordial Invitation

On the last day of the festival, the great day, while Jesus was standing there, he cried out, "Let anyone who is thirsty come to me, and let the one who believes in me drink. As the scripture has said, 'Out of the believer's heart shall flow rivers of living water.'" Now he said this about the Spirit, which believers in him were to receive; for as yet there was no Spirit, because Jesus was not yet glorified. (John 7:37–39)

The Christian religion is a personal religion. We are invited to share in a continuing personal relationship with our Lord. His invitation to us is altogether personal: "If anyone thirst, let him come to me."

The Master gives us himself. His Spirit is ever our Guide and Comforter. The Spirit of God is not some *thing*. Frequently we hear someone say, "When It is at work in our lives …." The Spirit of God is Someone. Therefore, he works personally with us, not manipulating us as if we were objects but loving us and affirming us as thinking, willing persons.

Therefore, let us respond positively to Christ's cordial invitation: "Come unto me."

Questions for Reflection

- Do you really believe in a personal God?
- If so, how personal?
- When thinking of God's invitation, do you think of responding to some distant, exalted deity or to a cherished friend?
- You know about God, but how well do you know God?

The Loving God

> Jesus straightened up and said to her, "Woman, where are they? Has no one condemned you?" She said, "No one, sir." And Jesus said, "Neither do I condemn you. Go your way, and from now on do not sin again." (John 8:10–11; see vs. 1–11)

What kind of treatment should sinners expect from God? Perhaps this familiar text provides us a clue. Obviously, God is not a great heavenly grandfather who does everything just the way we want him to perform. However, neither is he a great heavenly tyrant whose ultimate purpose is to terrorize us because of our sin and guilt. Such a concept of God is not based on biblical truth but rather on images of superstition and tradition.

Although God is sovereign, he is also loving. He is free from us, so he does that which is best for us. Accordingly, God enables us to confront our sin in the awareness that we indeed are sinners. Then he is free to forgive us our sin—not because he must do so, but because that is his desire. Such is the love of the loving sovereign God.

Questions for Reflection

> ➤ It is a sobering thought to consider that to ignore or reject the gift of God's love is to reject God himself.

- Have you considered the idea that to attempt to live with unforgiven sin is to struggle with a needless burden?
- To what extent is it true that our hesitancy to seek God's forgiveness is to retain the notion that we really are not bad people, and maybe our sins are, therefore, inconsequential?
- Why would any person reject the appeal of such a God of love?
- Remember Jesus's words: "Neither do I condemn you." Are you able to apply those words to yourself?

The Quest for Truth

> But because I tell the truth, you do not believe me. Which of you convicts me of sin? If I tell the truth, why do you not believe me? Whoever is from God hears the words of God. The reason that you do not hear them is that you are not from God. (John 8:45–47; see vs. 34–59)

The quest for truth is a common denominator in all people of all times. The intelligent person is willing to affirm that the quest frequently takes strange forms as it is traced throughout the pages of our common history. However, the intelligent Christian is one who has reached the conclusion that ultimate truth is personified in the face of Jesus of Nazareth.

After evaluating the respective offerings of the finest human contributions, the Christian is that person who is thoroughly convinced that Jesus Christ is the divine solution to the cosmic problems of life, death, eternity, suffering, sin, and judgment. In other words, Jesus Christ, as the dying and resurrected Lamb of God, is saving Truth. To know Jesus is the happy conclusion of our quest for truth.

The issue of truth was a central question in the trial of Jesus. Recall the discussion between Pilate and Jesus:

"For this I was born, and for this I came into the world, to testify to the truth. Everyone who belongs to the truth listens to my voice." Pilate asked him, "What is truth?" (John 18:37–38)

Questions for Reflection

- In light of the social unrest and the prevalent environment of negativity, which dominates any effort toward intelligent discourse, do you think that most of us are seriously searching for essential truth?
- What about that question Pilate raised? Why not try to answer that question for yourself? What is truth?
- Perhaps it will be instructive if we turn our attention to the insight of Jesus. He identified and defined truth for us: "I am … the truth …. No one comes to the Father except through me" (John 14:6).
- Our quest for truth, therefore, begins with and proceeds through the person and spirit of Jesus as Lord and First Cause of the entire created order.
- If our reflections on this matter are to be relevant, they must be personal. So be honest with yourself as never before. How do you feel about Jesus and his insights, principles, and examples? Remember that essential truth begins and ends with Jesus.

Community

> I have other sheep which do not belong to this fold. I must bring them also, and they will listen to my voice. So there will be one flock and one shepherd. (John 10:16; see vs. 11–18)

Community! That is a key word for Christian consideration. In fact, the survival of human civilization may well depend upon our gaining an awareness of the essential meaning inherent in the word *community*.

A typical understanding of community for most of us is limited to a rather circumscribed area or group. If we have an interest in achieving a Christian understanding, several important questions are appropriate: (1) What is essential for authentic human community to exist? (2) Can human community exist in such a diverse world as our own? (3) Can human community exist without a mutual faith in each person for each person, or without substantial hope for personal and corporate progress, or without love which retains the ability to affirm the ultimate worth of the other?

In a word, community is the objective of God for the human experience. The Christian stance must be unmistakable: We are one by creation and by redemption. We shall realize this objective as we actualize in all relationships those superlative virtues of faith, hope, and love.

Questions for Reflection

- Have you noted the volume of religious talk pertaining to the ideal of community?
- Have you also noted that within the environment of such religious talk there exists an abundance of prejudice and intolerance?
- In your thinking, to what extent do the divisive terms *African American, Asian American, Native American, European American*, etc., give emphasis to the principle of social separateness?
- Generally speaking, most of us enjoy sharing in the declaration that we are "one nation under God, with liberty and justice for all." Question: Are we really *one* nation? Really?

The Rediscovery of Christian Vitality

So again Jesus said to them, "Very truly, I tell you, I am the gate for the sheep. All who came before me are thieves and bandits; but the sheep did not listen to them. I am the gate. Whoever enters by me will be saved, and will come in and go out and find pasture. The thief comes only to steal and kill and destroy. I came that they may have life, and have it abundantly." (John 10:7–10)

Jesus spoke of abundant life: "I came that they might have life, and have it abundantly." What does this mean for us?

Each Christian is summoned to rediscover the excitement of Christian vitality. Far too many of us are guilty of taking a respite from the rigors of an aggressive and militant religious involvement. This has become a period of spiritual laxity and casual involvement.

A new day has dawned. We have been alerted to unprecedented opportunities for thoroughly Christian contributions in such varied areas as art and science, theology and politics, leisure activities and vocational routine. It is increasingly clear that we have reason to rejoice in this rediscovery of Christian vitality. One thing is certain: there is excitement, challenge, and reward in this adventure of rediscovery.

Questions for Reflection

- Do you feel excitement in your daily life?
- Are there times when you are aware of innovative and creative impulses in your conscious reflections?
- Are you allowing your Christian faith to influence your attitudes and actions?
- In other words, does your Christian faith really make a difference in your life?
- A challenge for you: Experience the exhilarating sense of joy that will come as you have a part in the start of a new redemptive adventure with your Lord.

I Can Face Tomorrow

> I am the resurrection and the life. Those who believe in me, even though they die, will live, and everyone who lives and believes in me will never die. Do you believe this? (John 11:25–26; see vs. 17–44)

We are acquainted with people who demonstrate the certain conviction that the best is yet to be. Often in life, we discover ourselves in the presence of those who are critically ill and, in some cases, dying. We may find ourselves surprised by the calm demeanor they have, and often they give witness to their faith that this is not for them the end. Rather, it is the beginning.

In light of this, there emerges in our own consciousness the conviction that the longer one knows the Master, walks with him, hears his words, and strives to follow his teachings, the more absolute the reality of God's eternal tomorrow becomes. Such thinking as this leaves us with an abiding impression:

> The streams on earth I've tasted,
> More deep I'll drink above;
> There, to an ocean fulness
> His mercy doth expand.
>
> —Anon.

Jesus said, "I am the resurrection and the life." This is our conviction! "Because he lives, I can face tomorrow!" Can you?

Questions for Reflection

- Generally speaking, are you a hopeful person?
- When the subject of the future is raised, do you experience fear?
- Anxiety?
- Anticipation?
- Peace?
- How does this relate to your Christian faith?
- Try this: In one paragraph, write your personal view of what heaven is really like.
- Is it true for you that the thought of God's tomorrow makes this a brighter and blessed day?

The Absence of Jesus

Jesus said, … "You always have the poor with you, but you do not always have me." (John 12:7–8; see vs. 1–8)

"You do not always have me." Those words were spoken by Jesus. They are strange to our ears because we are accustomed of thinking of Jesus as always being with us. Then he shocks us with the solemn declaration: "You do not always have me."

Does this mean that the Lord withdraws himself from us? Are there times in our lives when we must "go it alone"? If so, we had better cease our emphasis on the constant care and protection of the Savior. This cannot be! So what is the meaning?

For one thing, the time of our ability to serve the Lord is limited by our own humanity. Age, circumstance, and condition of health influence our capacity for spiritual service. It is not that Jesus forsakes us but rather that our opportunity for spiritual service is structured within the limitation of time and circumstance. Accordingly, whatever you will do for the Master, do it quickly.

Questions for Reflection

- Do you really believe that Jesus is always with you?
- That is the meaning of the word *Emmanuel*. But in light of your own experience, is he with you?
- Are there times when you feel forsaken by God?
- When are those times?
- How do you relate your own experience with the statement of Jesus, "You do not always have me with you"?
- Jesus also promised that "I will never leave you or forsake you." Do you feel comfort in this promise? Then respect his first statement, but let your faith rest in the second.

The Cross and the Towel

> During supper Jesus, knowing that the Father had given all things into his hands, and that he had come from God and was going to God, got up from the table, took off his outer robe, and tied a towel around himself. Then he poured water into a basin and began to wash the disciples' feet and to wipe them with the towel that was tied around him. (John 13:2–5; see vs. 1–20)

Many of us have difficulty with this passage. In a way, it is a little embarrassing to some of us. After all, what are we to do with it? Is this to be understood as a sacrament of the church the way baptism and the Lord's Supper are understood as sacraments? Should this be viewed as a rite of Christian worship in any sense of the word? Or should we do as we usually do, simply ignore it altogether?

Perhaps there is an often-overlooked answer to this frequently confusing issue. Recall the incident that occurred five days previously at another supper when Mary anointed the feet of Jesus. It should be noted that this actually was interpreted as preparation for the death of Jesus. Here Jesus anoints the feet of his disciples. The symbolism is consistent if we suggest that he was preparing them to lay down their lives for the sake of the gospel.

This raises an important question for us: Are we willing to have Christ wash our feet? You will note that when Peter protested Jesus washing his feet, the Master replied accordingly: "If I do not wash you, you have no part in me" (John 13:8 RSV).

Surely this important event reminds all Christians of the duty and privilege of laying down our lives for Christ and his kingdom. After all, we all give our lives to something. Why not the greatest Reality of all? Why not Christ and the cause of the kingdom? Well, now it is your move!

Questions for Reflection

- What meaning do you give to Christ washing the feet of his disciples?
- Are you willing to allow him to render the menial tasks required to cleanse yourself?
- Are you willing to allow any person to render such service to you?
- Are you willing to render the service to others?
- Explain what Jesus meant when he said, "If I do not wash you, you have no part in me."

Immortal Longings

Do not let your hearts be troubled. Believe in God, believe also in me. In my Father's house there are many dwelling places. If it were not so, would I have told you that I go to prepare a place for you? And if I go and prepare a place for you, I will come again and take you to myself, so that where I am, there you may be also. (John 14:1–3; see vs. 1–14)

Recall that last great act in Shakespeare's *Antony and Cleopatra*. Decked in the symbols of her former glory, the queen prepares for the end. Her words truly are prophetic:

> Give me my robe, put on my crown;
> I have immortal longings in me.

Surely each of us is endowed with such "immortal longings." We feel deeply that we were created for life, not death. Therefore, we strive for life!

Jesus said, "I am the life." To know Jesus as Savior now is to know him then as well. There is no assurance of life, eternal and qualitative life, other than Jesus. In Jesus there is the divine vitality that sustains us now and will vitalize us through all eternity.

The grandeur and mystery of immortality is impossible to fully understand or explain. The thoughts of Henry Vaughan (1622–1695) provide needed light on the subject:

> Dear beauteous death! The Jewel of the Just,
> Shining no where, but in the dark;
> What mysteries do lie beyond thy dust,
>   Could man outlook that mark!

Questions for Reflection

- Do you think often of heaven and the hereafter?
- Are you fearful or expectant when reflecting on such ideas?
- Consider John 11:25–26:

  > Jesus said to her, "I am the resurrection and the life. Those who believe in me, even though they die, will live, and everyone who lives and believes in me will never die. Do you believe this?"

- Do *you* believe this?

Christ's Peace

> I have said these things to you while I am still with you. But the Advocate, the Holy Spirit, whom the Father will send in my name, will teach you everything and remind you of all that I have said to you. Peace I leave with you; my peace I give to you. I do not give to you as the world gives. Do not let your hearts be troubled, and do not let them be afraid. (John 14:25–27)

There is much talk these days about the importance of every person preparing a will. Indeed, that is an essential responsibility which none of us should shirk. We Christians are blessed to discover that Jesus declared his Last Will and Testament: "Peace I leave with you. My peace I give to you."

Personal serenity escapes many of us these days. In our seasons of distress and worry, the prayer of Whittier is most appropriate:

> Take from our souls the strain and stress,
> And let our ordered lives confess
> The beauty of Thy peace.

The peace of Christ is available for each of us, and it is available today. His peace is not lethargic and passive.

Rather, it is the stalwart protector of the believing soul whose affection truly is set on Jesus.

Questions for Reflection

- What do you think is the secret to an anxiety-free life?
- Think again what it means to have the Holy Spirit dwelling within you. What is it that he can and will do for you?
- Paul advises us to "be filled with the Holy Spirit." Consider the idea that if one is filled (emphasis on filled) with the Holy Spirit, there is no room for fear, anxiety, bitterness, or any sense of failure. And just think! Such is our inheritance as children of God.
- So just reflect on it. If this gift of Christ is so great, why would anyone hesitate to invite the Spirit of Christ into his heart? Well?

How to Choose a Friend

> I do not call you servants any longer, because the servant does not know what the master is doing, but I have called you friends, because I have made known to you everything I have heard from my Father. You did not choose me but I chose you. And I appoint you to go and bear fruit, fruit that will last, so that my Father will give you whatever you ask him in my name. I am giving you these commands so that you may love one another. (John 15:15–17; see vs. 1–17)

Among our social conventions there may be found many safeguards against the possible "wrong" friends. One such oracle of truth declares: "If you lie down with dogs, you'll rise up with fleas." Another gem of wisdom declares: "Birds of a feather always flock together." The moral of such views is that the intelligent person will carefully choose friends to retain one's present social status and even advance one's social position if possible. In other words, we are under social pressure to climb the social ladder.

Where does such thinking leave the Christian? If we forever reach out to those socially elite individuals who already have so many friends that they have no special need for us, what happens to the ignored and forgotten among us? Surely, we reject that idiotic idiom, "Everyone must look out for Number One." There is a Christian way to choose a friend, and Charles F. Brown has put it to verse:

> Reach out and touch a friend who is weary;
>   reach out and touch a seeker unaware;
> Reach out and touch, though touching means losing
>   a part of your own self—if you dare!
> Reach out and give your love to the loveless;
> Reach out and make a home for the homeless;
>   Reach out and shed God's light in the darkness!
>   Reach out and let the smile of God touch thro' you.

Questions for Reflection

- Jesus was identified as a friend of sinners. Are you so identified? Should you be?
- Can you make a list of five people whom you call friends who might be considered by others as "real sinners"?
- It is noted that Jesus chose his friends from the "wrong crowd." What would he think of your choice of friends?
- Think deeply for a moment. What is your motivation in your choice of friends?

The Spirit of Truth

> I still have many things to say to you, but you cannot bear them now. When the Spirit of truth comes, he will guide you into all the truth for he will not speak on his own, but will speak whatever he hears, and he will declare to you the things that are to come. He will glorify me, for he will take what is mine and declare it to you. All that the Father has is mine. For this reason I said that I will take what is mine and declare it to you. (John 16:12–15)

The Christian is the recipient of that new quality of life which is known as eternal life. Eternal life is God-given and is the very life of God himself. Thus, eternal life for the Christian is the personal realization of the presence of God. The presence of God in the life of the Christian is most frequently called Holy Spirit.

To live and walk in God's presence is to experience Holy Spirit. Such experience is to be desired, not feared. It is beneficial, not detrimental. It is beautiful, not awesome. It is creative, not destructive. Therefore, the blessing of Holy Spirit in one's life is God's best gift to the Christian.

The privilege of the Christian is that of abiding in the reality and presence of God himself. That the Holy Spirit is available for such constant encouragement, instruction, and fellowship for us is the continuing gift of God. To make the practice of utter and complete dependence upon the Comforter a long-standing habit is to render impotent the great enemies of humankind. Those defeated enemies are emptiness, guilt and death.

Questions for Reflection

> ➤ Think about yourself for a moment. Think about yourself as if you were a house (2 Corinthians 5:1–5).
> ➤ Consider that two people live in the house that is your physical being. These two people are you and the Holy Spirit.
> ➤ Question: Who is in charge in your house?

Victory in Jesus

I have said this to you, so that in me you may have peace. In the world you face persecution. But take courage; I have conquered the world. (John 16:33; see vs. 29–33)

Jesus said, "I have conquered the world!" That startling declaration became fact as with his dying breath on the cross Jesus gave the victor's shout, "It is finished!" The decisive battle has been won. Practically, the war is over. A few skirmishes continue to mar the reign of the Prince of Peace, but they will soon cease. Death, sin, and Satan are forever defeated. Contrary to the title of a popular book, *There's a New World Coming*, the new world is here already! The anthem of the believer is not "The King is coming." Rather, the anthem is the victory shout of the Christian: "Christ reigns!"

We freely admit that we remain in the world, and the world is very much with us. Yet we no longer fear the darkness for we have seen the face of God. We have looked into the face of Jesus and have seen love and grace. And we know that we are saved and safe, for he is our King.

Why are there days in which we mooch along in the foreboding flatlands between anxiety on one hand and despair on the other? Why do we permit the apparent obstacles of life to thwart our best efforts? When we think about it, really think about it, we are confident in the ultimate realization of God's purpose in our lives. After all, we have Christ's uplifting promise, "Take courage; I have conquered the world!"

Questions for Reflection

- What do you do when you feel that you have reached the limits of your capacity and still face insurmountable problems?
- What role does your religious faith play in your life at such times?
- Think about today. Any problems you are dreading?
- Are you able to apply today's text to today's tasks?
- Now focus your attention on at least one area of your life in which you are certain of success, peace, and, especially, victory.
- Are you not able to realize the reality of Christ's declaration, "I have conquered the world"?

Eternal Life

> And this is eternal life, that they may know you, the only true God, and Jesus Christ whom you have sent. (John 17:3, see vs. 1–5)

They are at it again! The proponents of the notion that perpetual youth is a possibility are at it again! We are being told that notwithstanding the passing of the years, it is possible to look young and feel young indefinitely. One wonders.

What is there about the human mentality that motivates us to think in terms of extended longevity? It seems that there is built into the very fiber of our beings the notion of immortality. It is as if our very nature cries out that we were born to live, not die. Is such extended life possible?

Jesus of Nazareth taught that eternal life is a reality. Notice how he phrased the matter: "This is life eternal, that they might know you, the only true God, and Jesus Christ whom you have sent." Now that is a new insight. Eternal life is perfect knowledge of God, which is possible through a right relationship with Jesus Christ. See! You can live forever if you choose to live in Christ. Longfellow summarizes well our Christian faith in this regard:

Life is real! Life is earnest!
And the grave is not its goal;
Dust thou art, to dust returnest,
Was not spoken of the soul.

Questions for Reflection

- Are you unnerved by the thought of death?
- Do you consider death to be the end of life?
- What meaning do you give to the idea of resurrection?
- Consider these lines of Robert Freeman and whether they reflect your own faith:

> Shall I doubt my Father's mercy?
> Shall I think of death as doom,
> Or the stepping o'er the threshold
> Of a bigger, brighter room?

Eternal Life II

> And this is eternal life, that they may know you, the only true God, and Jesus Christ whom you have sent. (John 17:3, see vs. 1–5)

It is strange how perceptions change with the passing of time. For the very young, it seems an eternity from one Christmas to the next. Not so for the mature adult, who feels at times as if the year contained only brief moments, not months. Further, the very young tend to view the future in terms of anticipated activities and achievements. In contrast, the very old tend to view the future with an awareness of terminal certitude.

It is little wonder that the passing of time is accompanied with a steadily growing appreciation of the nature and meaning of life. And through it all there remains that inexplicable and universal conviction that life transcends time. Jesus of Nazareth spoke often of eternal life. His observations forever are credible because of one singular event—his resurrection from the dead. So when he speaks, we listen:

> I am the resurrection and the life;
> he who believes in me, though he die,
> yet shall he live, and whoever lives
> and believes in me shall never die.
> (John 11:25–26)

Questions for Reflection

- How do you view the future?
- When thinking of such things, do you linger on events or persons?
- Do you have unquestioned faith in the veracity of the resurrection of Jesus?
- To what extent does this component of your faith system influence your own confidence and hope of eternal life?
- Consider the words penned by William Gaither and reflect on whether or not they represent your own personal faith:

> Because He lives I can face tomorrow,
> Because He lives all fear is gone;
> Because I know He holds the future,
> And life is worth the living just because
> He lives.

Truth

Pilate asked him, "So you are a king?" Jesus answered, "You say that I am a king. For this I was born, and for this I came into the world, to testify to the truth. Everyone who belongs to the truth listens to my voice." Pilate asked him, "What is truth?" (John 18:37–38; see vs. 33–38)

Pilate asked the question, "What is truth?" Jesus gave the answer, "I am the truth." It is regrettable for Pilate that he was unaware that it was Truth to whom he posed the question. How altogether human!

Each of us can sympathize with Pilate because each of us has stood in his shoes at one time or another. Like Pilate, we have wondered what to do next. And like Pilate, we, too, often have erred in our choices and actions. Is it not strange that frequently we who know the Truth fail to act accordingly?

Have we as yet arrived to a precise answer to Pilate's question? Perhaps the following will prove adequate for the occasion: "Truth is a quality of judgment reached as a result of the total witness of fact and individual and collective experience" (*Looking Ahead*, p. 151).

Questions for Reflection

- Let us begin our reflections with the following prayer:

  > Lord Jesus, we know you to be the way, the truth, and the life. Help us to so live the truth that it becomes for us the way of life. To the glory of your name we pray. Amen.

- In this world of uncertainties and variables, how does one determine the truth?
- Why do we sometimes look at the truth and yet fail to recognize it as such?
- Is it possible that I am missing some obvious truth today?
- Am I faithful to retain Jesus Christ central to my thoughts and actions?

King of Kings

Now it was the day of Preparation for the Passover; and it was about noon. He said to the Jews, "Here is your King!" They cried out, "Away with him! Away with him! Crucify him!" Pilate asked them, "Shall I crucify your King?" The chief priests answered, "We have no king but the emperor." Then he handed him over to them to be crucified. (John 19:14–16; see vs. 12–16)

Whether he knew it or not, the words of Pontius Pilate were prophetic for all of humanity: *Behold your king!* Ever since that turbulent hour, Jesus has been recipient of a unique designation by Christian faith, a designation which is unique in kind from that of any other person. He is believed to be both Lord of lords and King of kings.

So we give to our King this unrivaled place because we know that he has assumed for himself this rightful place. Ultimately, we are certain, the entire universe will acknowledge his sovereignty. After all, here is the record: "And the Lamb shall overcome them: for he is Lord of lords and King of kings."

We have just given emphasis to one of the most important and relevant components of our common faith. In times like these in which we live, often wondering if there is any hope for our world, the sovereignty of Jesus Christ is our assurance. It is good to realize that in a time when we are in desperate need of true leadership in our nation and world, we have that great Leader – our Lord Jesus Christ!

Questions for Reflection

- Talk of the Lordship of Jesus is good news. But is it real?
- Is Jesus really in charge of world affairs today?
- If so, why the global turmoil which afflicts us all?
- Let us narrow the discussion. What about your own personal life?
- Is Jesus in charge?
- Are you permitting him to reign in your life? In everything?
- Is this not the perfect moment for you to surrender your life to the Lordship of Jesus Christ?

The Cross of Christ

> So they took Jesus; and carrying the cross by himself, he went to what is called The Place of the Skull, which in Hebrew is called Golgotha. There they crucified him, and with him two others, one on either side, with Jesus between them. (John 19:16–18; see vs. 16–25)

Christians are a peculiar lot. With so much in the world that is beautiful, we have given most of our emphasis to the execution of a condemned man which took place by crucifixion two thousand years ago. What was there about that event that set people thinking in a way they had never thought previously? After all, more books have been written about that execution, more pictures painted about that victim on the cross, and more lives have been committed to the cause espoused by the crucified man from Nazareth than can be enumerated. As a matter of fact, the image of that cross remains central to our religion. Why should it be so?

Allow the New Testament to answer the question:

> God commendeth his love toward us, in that, while we were yet sinners, Christ died for us. (Romans 5:8 KJV)

> God so loved the world that he gave his only son. (John 3:16)

> In this is love, not that we loved God but that he loved us and sent his Son to be the atoning sacrifice for our sins. (1 John 4:10)

That is the reason for the centrality of the cross in our Christian faith. Let us ever say with Paul, "May I never boast of anything except the cross of our Lord Jesus Christ" (Galatians 6:14).

Questions for Reflection

- Do you find it difficult to comprehend the idea of God being a victim?
- Are you able to fathom the thought of the death of God?
- To what extent are you able to understand how you are personally involved in Christ's death?
- Do you ever seriously reflect on the fact that Jesus died for *your* sins?
- Does such thinking leave you with any sense of guilt?
- Assimilate into your own experience the words of the familiar spiritual: "Were you there when they crucified my Lord?" Well, were you?

Human Needs

> After this, when Jesus knew that all was now finished, he said (in order to fulfill the scripture), "I am thirsty." A jar full of sour wine was standing there. So they put a sponge full of the wine on a branch of hyssop and held it to his mouth. When Jesus had received the wine, he said, "It is finished." Then he bowed his head and gave up his spirit. (John 19:28–30)

The saying of our Lord, "I thirst," indicates the body has its rights. While in the light of Christ's example, these rights must be restrained, subordinated, and held in check, they are legitimate in their own place and in due measure. This is of great value to us because Jesus identified with our problem, which is far better than merely offering us some kind of super solution. And that identifying with us is what he did throughout his life.

Come to think of it, he identified with us so completely that the Pharisees mistook him for a sinner. The point is that he trusted himself and his plight into the hands of others. He confessed his need! One wonders why we trap our needs, our pains, and our confusions within ourselves. Therefore, we become victims to our own inordinate restraint. Perhaps we could, with considerable profit, apply the words of the familiar hymn, "I Need Thee Every Hour," as our personal petition:

I need Thee every hour, most gracious Lord;
No tender voice like Thine can peace afford.
I need Thee, O I need Thee;
Every hour I need Thee.

Questions for Reflection

- How are things with you today?
- What hurt have you trapped within the recesses of your being that is threatening your potential for a full and meaningful life?
- Have you discussed the matter with a loved one, a friend, or even God?
- If within you there is something broken (e.g., a relationship, a financial problem, or a health problem). Consider taking it to a friend, a counselor, a minister, or surely to God.
- Do you realize that you will be greatly blessed if that which is broken is completely mended?
- Ultimately try this: "Take your burden (need) to the Lord, and leave it there."

The Christian and Missions

Jesus said to them again, "Peace be with you. As the Father has sent me, so I send you." (John 20:21; see vs. 19–23)

The matter of missions is not an issue to be decided by the church. The Great Commission is a mandate from God. Any ignoring of missions is a flagrant disobedience. Our Lord has directed that we are to go, to preach, and make disciples. Still, the question is often raised, "Why bother with missions?"

We bother with missions because the Christ-event remains the greatest news of the ages. We bother with missions because we know that the gospel of Christ is the only sufficient answer to the needs of humanity. We bother with missions because it is the inherent right of every person to know what God has done for him. We bother with missions because we are certain that when our witness ceases, the church of Jesus Christ will have failed to be the church of Jesus Christ.

The personal imperative of Christian missions confronts each of us. There is that unavoidable declaration of the commissioning Christ: "As my Father has sent me, so I send you." If we are Christians, missions remains our ultimate responsibility. May God help us to accept Christ's challenge and share the gospel with the whole world in this generation.

Questions for Reflection

- Until now, have you fully understood the meaning of the word *missions*?
- Are you willing to comply with its mandate in your own life?
- In what concrete ways can and will you respond to the call and claim of Christ in your life?
- Are you willing to offer God the following prayer-and mean it? Just think about this prayer:

> Lord Jesus:
> I'll do what you want me to do.
> I'll go where you want me to go.
> I'll be what you want me to be.
> Amen.

Honest Skepticism

> But Thomas (who was called the Twin), one of the twelve, was not with them when Jesus came. So the other disciples told him, "We have seen the Lord." But he said to them, "Unless I see the mark of the nails in his hands, and put my finger in the mark of the nails, and my hand in his side, I will not believe." (John 20:24–25; see vs. 19–29)

Although frequently we are urged to refrain from questioning the works and ways of God, it will be well for us to note the value of honest skepticism. Actually, it is not foreign to Christian faith to ask the question, "Why?" Recall Jesus doing just that as he suffered on the cross: "My God, my God, why have you forsaken me?"

It is difficult to comprehend that in this age of enlightenment we should negate the positive benefit of the questioning mentality. Rather, we should celebrate the intellectual courage of those thinkers of the past and present who have dared to be open-minded enough for God to pour new life and new truth into the human experience.

Come to think of it, some significant questions are being asked in our time: Why must innocent children languish in poverty? Why must we be subject to cancer and coronary arrest? Why must there be war again and again and again?

Such questions, if honestly dealt with, leave us open to receive truth, redemptive truth, God's truth.

Questions for Reflection

- Do you challenge your faith by allowing the big questions to be raised?
- If you are relatively comfortable and are "making it" in life, are you satisfied to accept things as they are?
- When you see human suffering, ignorance, disease, poverty, child abuse, and a host of other social ills, do you confront your God with the big question, "Why?"
- If not, why not?
- Regarding your personal faith system, are you aware that skepticism is not a refutation of Christian conviction?
- In his initial response to the reports of Jesus's resurrection, Thomas said in effect, "I'll have to see it to believe it!" As a result, Jesus showed him!
- Now, reflect on ways that honest skepticism can result in positive and redemptive results.